Stories from HIGHLANDS NEW JERSEY

Stories from HIGHLANDS NEW JERSEY

A Sea of Memories

EDITED BY JOHN P. KING

THE History PRESS

Published by The History Press
Charleston, SC 29403
www.historypress.net

Unless otherwise noted, all images appear courtesy of the author.

First published 2012

Manufactured in the United States

ISBN 978.1.60949.707.1

Library of Congress CIP data applied for.

Notice: The information in this book is true and complete to the best of our knowledge. It is offered without guarantee on the part of the author or The History Press. The author and The History Press disclaim all liability in connection with the use of this book.

Joan Brady Wicklund.

Dedicated to Joan Wicklund
ever a good friend
to the Town and all people
of Highlands.

In Memoriam
John Tomasulo
1953–2001
a big man with an even bigger heart
filled and overflowing
with a love of Highlands and its history
and with genuine goodness.

John Tomasulo, 1953–2001.

Contents

Contents

Highlands is indeed a town embraced by the sea, unique among all other towns on the bay and rivers.

Introduction

Highlands, New Jersey, is a town embraced by the sea that has used its location defined by hills, ocean, bay and river to grow in importance as a shell fishing and resort community well before its inception as a borough in 1900. Despite economic and developmental setbacks over the years and all too frequent floods in times of storms, Highlands remains strong and prosperous in recent years, always a proud, hardworking and close-knit community.

Stories from Highlands, New Jersey: A Sea of Memories is an anthology of original history, a collection of spoken and written images that permit the reader to experience the speaker's or writer's views, impressions and opinions of life in town and to appreciate the character and spirit of the land and people of Highlands. Over fifty pictures, many not previously published, illustrate the words of the speakers and writers who were and are everyday people remembering and telling us their view of the history of Highlands. These historians allow us to preserve for the future images of a land and a life in the past, things that have passed away and things that remain today much as they always were. Everyone has a story to tell; they only need someone to willing to listen.

A Personal Introduction

I have many friends who are collectors. Some collect stamps, dolls, coins or small china objects. I have always been tolerant of this hobby, but not really interested.

Suddenly I realize that I, too, am a collector. I collect memories. And what a collection I have. Some are trivial, some are ridiculous, some heart-warming and some too endearing to share. But all are good. The unpleasant ones I banish. Who has room for those?

These memories influence my moods, my attitude and even my life. I can reach in and pull out the right one whenever I need it to sustain me. If I'm feeling down, I have only to think of a little mouse washing his face, and I'm smiling again. No one who has ever seen such a performance can ever forget it.

—Ann McNeill,

Who had an undying love affair with Highlands, never tiring of talking and writing about Highlands in the nineteenth and twentieth centuries. Blessed with charm, sweetness and a keen mind, she delighted in sharing her memories of life in Highlands with everyone.

Inset, above: Ann McNeill, confined to a wheel chair and a bit deaf but with her same outgoing charm and lucidity, as she celebrated her ninety-ninth birthday and was named Monmouth County Poet Laureate in Highlands Borough Hall.

Part 1

Our Earliest Memories

The Coming of the White Man

The Lenape Indians of the Highlands area did not possess a written language and depended upon oral tradition to preserve the records of events, passing down into each generation stories like the following, which ultimately was written for them in 1819 by John Heckewelder.

A long time before men with a white skin had ever been seen, some Indians fishing at a place where the sea widens espied something at a distance moving upon the water. They hurried ashore, collected their neighbors, who together returned and viewed intently this astonishing phenomenon.

What it could be baffled conjecture. Some supposed it to be a large fish or other animal; others thought it was a large house floating on the sea. Perceiving it moving toward the land, the spectators concluded that it would be proper to send runners in different directions to carry the news to their scattered chiefs, that they might send off for the immediate attendance of their warriors.

These arrived in numbers to behold the sight, and perceiving that it was actually moving toward them, that it was coming into the bay, they conjectured that it must be a remarkably large house in which the Manito or Great Spirit was coming to visit them. They were much afraid, yet under no apprehension that the great spirit would injure them.

A group of Lenape watch in awe and dread at the coming of the *Half Moon*, wondering what this event portended for their life and people, on September 2, 1609.

The chiefs assembled at New York Island and consulted in what manner they should receive their Manito. Meat was prepared for a sacrifice. Utterly at a loss as to what to do and distracted alternately between hope and fear, in the confusion a great dance was begun.

In the meantime fresh runners arrived, declaring it to be a great house of various colors and full of living creatures. Others arriving declared it positively full of people, of different color and dress from them and that one appeared altogether in red. This must be the Manito. They were lost in admiration, could not imagine why the vessel was, or what all this portended for them.

They are now hailed from the vessel in a language they could not understand. They answered by a shout or a yell in their own way. The house stops. A small canoe comes onshore with the red man in it. The chief and wise men formed a circle into which the red man and two attendants enter. He salutes them with friendly countenance, and they returned the salute after their manner.

They are amazed at their color and their dress, especially him. He must be a great Manito, they thought, but why should he have a white skin? And what does all this portend for the Lenape?

—Lenape account, recorded by Reverend John Heckewelder, 1819

A Further Account of New Jersey

The following description of life in Highlands in 1675, the oldest we have, was written as a Proprietary propaganda piece in the form of a genuine letter in order to entice other settlers to leave England and settle in New Jersey.

A FURTHER ACCOUNT OF NEW JERSEY IN AN ABSTRACT OF LETTERS LATELY WRIT FROM THENCE BY SEVERAL INHABITANTS THERE RESIDENT

Dear Friend:

My love is to thee and to thy wife, desiring your welfare, both inward and outward; and that we may be found steadfast in that truth which is saving, for the welfare of our immortal souls. And, dear friend, the desire of my soul is, that we may know true love; and I shall be glad to see thee and thy wife. I have a partly remembrance of thy wife. And I have thought of thee many times with tears in my eyes. The Lord has done wondrous works for me: unto Him return thanks and praises, who is God over all Blessed forever.

Now, friend, I shall give some information concerning New Jersie, but time will not permit me to write at length. Thee desireth to know how I live. Through the goodness of the Lord I live very well, keeping between thirty and forty head of cows and seven or eight horses to ride upon.

There are several towns settled in this Province, viz., Shrewsbury, and Middletown, upon the Sea Side, and along the river side, and up the creek there is Piscattaway and Woodbridge, Elizabethtown, New Coake and Bergen. Most of these Towns have about one hundred families; and the least forty. The country is very beautiful.

In Middletown, where I live, in six years and upwards there have died but one woman about eighty years old, one man about sixty, and a boy about five years old, and one little infant or two. There are in this Town, in twenty-five families about ninety-five children, most of them under twelve years of age, and all lusty children.

The produce of this Provence is chiefly, Wheat, Barley Oates, Beans, Beef, Pork, Pease, Tobacco, Indian corn, Butter, Cheese, hemp and flax, French beans, Strawberries, Carrots, Parsnips, Cabbidge, Turnips, Radishes, Onions, Cucumbers, Watermellons, Mushmellons, Squashes; also our soile is verry fertile for Apples, Pears, Plums, Quinces, Currans red and white,

Gooseberries, Cherries and Peaches in abundance, having all sorts of green trash in the summer time.

The Country is greatly supplied with Creeks and Rivers, which afford stores of Fish, Pearch, Roach, Baste, Sheepsheads, Oysters, Crabs, Sturgeons, Eels and many other sorts of Fish that I do not name. You may buy as much Fish of an Indian for half a pound of Powder as will serve six or eight men.

Deer are also very plenty in this Province. We can buy a fat Buck of the Indians much bigger than the English Deer for a pound and a half of Powder or Lead or any other trade equivalent; and a peck of Strawberries, the Indians will gather and bring Home to us for the value of six pence.

Our Beef and Pork is verry fat and good. The natural Grass of the country is much like that which grows in the Woods in England, which is food enough for our Cattle; but by the water side we have fresh meadows Salt Marshes. We make English Bread and Beer; besides we have several sorts of other Drink.

In traveling in the Country and coming to any House, they generally ask you to eat and drink, and take Tobacco, and their several sorts of Drink they will offer you as confidently as if it were Sack.

Here are abundance of Chestnuts, Walnuts, Mulberries and Grapes, red and white. Our Horses and Mares run in the open Woods, and we give them no meal Winter nor Summer, unless we work them; but our cows must be looked after.

Our Timber Stands for fences about the Land we manure; we Plough our land with oxen for the most part. Husbandman here and in Old England is all one, making most of our utencils for Husbandry ourselves, and a man that has three or four sonns or servants that can work along with him will down with Timber and get corn quickly.

The best coming to this country is at the Spring or Fall. We make our soap and candles and all such things ourselves. In the Winter we make good fires and we eat good Meat; and our women and children are healthy; sugar is cheap, venisan, Geese, turkeys, Pidgeons, Fowls and Fish are plenty and one great happiness we enjoy, which is we are very quiet.

I could give thee more information concerning this country but time will not give leave. In short, this is a rare place for any poor man, or others: and I am satisfied that people can live better here than they can in Old England, and eat more good meat. The vessel is going away, I have no time to copy this over, therefore take the sense of it. My love salutes thee. Farewell.

—Richard Hartshorne, New Jersie, Middleton, 12th of 9th Month 1675

The Indians Came to My House

The Hartshorne house at Portland on the other side of the peninsula from Highlands (Portland Road led to it.) had always been a prominent landmark known to the small English, Dutch and Lenape population living in and around Highlands. The house and farms are first mentioned due to the threats Hartshorne encountered from the native Indians there.

Lappawinsoe, Lenape chief of West New Jersey, pictured in 1737, after the population of Lenape dwindled from two thousand to about five hundred. Accurately painted by Granville Penn, it is representative of how Vowavapon and Tucus, who sold lands to Richard Hartshorne in 1678, would have looked.

The Indians came to my house and laid their hands on the post and frame of the house and said that the house was theirs, that they had never had anything for it and they told me that if I would not buy the land, I must be gone…They at last told me that they would kill my cattle and burn my hay, if I would not buy the land or be gone. Then I went to the Patentee office…;they told me that it was never bought nor had the Indians anything for it.

—Richard Hartshorne, 1678

Sold for Thirteen Shillings

These same Lenape Indians of the Highlands came into dispute with Hartshorne over access by them to the natural resources of Sandy Hook and the Highlands peninsula. One issue was their fishing and harvesting of beach plums each September and October, a right most Highlanders were denied by Fort Hancock authorities from time to time.

Whereas the Indians pretend that formerly, when they sold all the land on Sandy Hook, they did not sell or did except liberty to get beach plumbs, or to say the Indians have liberty to go on Sandy Hook to get plumbs when they please, and to hunt upon the land and fish and take dry trees that suited them for canoes.

A historical sketch by William Canfield shows Lenape Vowavapon and Tocus agreeing to sell Richard Hartshorne all rights to Sandy Hook.

Now know all men by these presents that I, Richard Hartshorne, of Portland, in the county of Monmouth, in East Jersey, for peace and quietness sake, and to the end that there may not be cause of trouble with these Indians, and that I may not for the future have any trouble with them as I formerly had, in their dogs killing my sheep and their hunting on my lands, and their fishing, I have agreed as followeth:

These presents witnesseth that I, Vowavapon, Hendricks, the Indians sonn, having all the liberty and privileges of pluming on Sandy Hook, hunting, fishing, fowling, getting cannows, etc., by these presents, give, grant, and bargain, sell unto Richard Hartshorne, his heirs, and assigns forever, all the liberty and privileges of pluming, fishing, fouling, hunting and whatsoever reserved and excepted by the Indians, for him, the said Richard Hartshorn, his heirs and assigns forever to have, hold, possess, and enjoy forever, to say that no Indian or Indians shall or hath no pretense to lands or timbers, liberty, privileges, on no pretense whatsoever on any part and parcel of land, belonging to the said Richard Hartshorne, to say Sandy Hook or land adjoining it, in consideration the said Richard Hartshorn hath paid unto the said Vowavapon thirteen shillings money; and I, the said Vowavapon do acknowledge to have received thirteen shillings by these presents witness my hand and seal.

Signed, sealed and delivered in the presence of John Stout.

Vowavapon X (his mark)
Tocus X (his mark)

Richard Hartshorne
8 August, 1678

Old Times in Highlands

Mrs. Eleanor Thompson Benton of Brooklyn, daughter of hotelier Joseph Thompson, founder of Thompson's Pavilion, was a former resident of Highlands who, at age eighty-five, shared her keen memory of Highlands life in a letter addressed to a local newspaper.

I came to Highlands in 1846, when a child, moving from a farm near Freehold. Sandy Hook at that time was an island, there being no beach opposite Highlands as at present. The old Ocean House hotel, which was destroyed by fire May 20, 1862, stood on the northernmost part of the peninsula, which now forms the larger part of the Borough of Sea Bright. A beach was made up in 1848, which joined the island of Sandy Hook with the mainland.

The steamer *Orus*, plying between New York and Long Branch, made regular stops for passengers. All persons going to New York has to cross the river to the Ocean House at Rocky Point and then take the steamboat. I took my first trip to New York on the *Orus*, going outside of Sandy Hook through the inlet opposite Island Beach (now called Plum Island), and well remember how I lay seasick on the cabin floor until I reached New York.

The Highlands, when I first knew it, consisted of four houses and a signal telegraph house. Colonel Jones of New York bought the Water Witch property in the early fifties. It was the scene of J. Fenimore Cooper's novel *Water Witch*, and the old school house referred to in Cooper's novel was used for a time as a private school. I was a pupil in that school. There was no public school at Highlands at that time. The building was later destroyed by fire. Subsequently the Water Witch property was divided into residential sites.

The house I lived in at Highlands was bought by my father from the Hartshorne estate. It was once occupied by an old Indian doctor. It is nearly two hundred years old. My father enlarged this building in 1854. It is now occupied by A.P. Riker and his sister. I saw the cornerstone laid at the present lighthouse, which was built in 1862. Part of the Highlands took on the name Parkertown, this being caused by a large number of families named Parker coming into that section. This part of Highlands was largely submerged at high tides.

I cannot describe the rejoicing that came upon us when the first railroad was built on the beach at Sandy Hook. The government dock was built in 1860–61. When the war broke out in '61, 500 or more soldiers were stationed at Sandy Hook, and the government built barracks for them there, but after the battle of Bull Run, most of them were removed. I walked on the government dock before it was finished to board the *Highland Light*, a steamboat running to Red Bank.

In 1857, all water communication between New York and this part of New Jersey was cut off. The river and the bay were frozen beyond Sandy Hook Point. The only way to New York was by the stage line through the Amboys. Transportation facilities were mostly by water or by stage at that time until the old Southern Railroad was built with its terminal at Port Monmouth.

The winter of 1857 was the most severe that I can ever remember. Sleighing parties went from Highlands to Red Bank on the ice on the river, and that winter I took my first iceboat sail, going from Highlands to Red Bank.

Highlands has been the scene of many historical and spectacular incidents. The ship *North America* was wrecked on the shoals opposite Island Beach, and well I remember how I played on its decks. The wrecking crews removed what was left of the vessel in 1848. When this boat floundered, 510 persons were lost and 89 were saved.

Another shipwreck that happened below Long Branch was that of the German immigrant vessel *New Era*. The coast was strewn with dead bodies,

The James McGarry house, where Ann McNeill was born and grew up, is the second-oldest house in Highlands, built in 1856, at 179 Navesink Avenue.

and folks went from Highlands to Long Branch with carts and wagons to help remove and bury these bodies. I saw nine dead bodies on the beach one morning.

The burning of the hotel Sea View was another incident to which my memory reverts. This fire occurred shortly after Donnelly, the hotel bookkeeper, killed a clerk called Moses.

An incident that brought many people to Highlands was the death of two large whales which lost their way in the Shrewsbury River in the early 1850s. They got on a sand bar opposite the Highlands, where they died. They were floated across to Highlands, where they were placed in a large tent, and sightseers had to pay to look at them. They were later floated to "Greenland" about a mile from Water Witch and made into fertilizer. I remember having taken a bath in the river where the whales were exhibited.

—Eleanor Thompson Benton

Part 2

Getting Here and Around

Transportation

Transportation has certainly changed over the years.

I loved the trains, big, noisy and exciting. Their whistles announced the time of day or night. Somehow it was comforting to wake in the night to its "whoo-whoo" as it passed through town under the hill.

Two sets of paddle wheelers plied the rivers. The *Mary Patten*, *Thomas Patten*, *Little Silver* and *Elberon* sailed down one branch of the river to Pleasure Bay, in Long Branch; the *Albertina* and the *Sea Bird* took the other branch to Red Bank.

What a beautiful sail it was to Red Bank. Mother and I would catch the boat at eleven o'clock and after a couple of stops would reach Red Bank at noon. The first thing that we did was have lunch in a restaurant on Front Street. I always had steak and French fries and felt so grown up. After lunch we made a short visit to Uncle Tom's. Then we returned to town to do our shopping. We caught the four o'clock boat back home arriving at five very contented with our day.

—Ann McNeill

THE TROLLEY

The trolley operated from September 1907 to 1923.

The trolley company was the Jersey Central Traction Co. The line ran from Perth Amboy down to South Jersey, through South Amboy and Sayreville, into Union Beach, Keansburg and Campbell's Junction at Belford. They had two lines from Campbell's Junction, one went to Red Bank and the other line came down along Valley Drive and got to Atlantic Highlands. Then it went to the Stone Church and came up Navesink Ave. to Route 36 in the Highlands. It made a right turn at Portland Rd.

—G. Lester Whitfield

TOO MANY STOPS

My first recollection of the Highlands was going with my grandmother to visit her brother's widow and her nephews in 1916 when I was five years old. We went in an open-air trolley from Long Branch to Red Bank, where we changed to the Highlands line via Campbell's Junction, and somehow, we landed there. All I remember was that it was a very long ride, and the trolley made too many stops.

My next early memory of the Highlands was from the Sandy Hook steamers and the boat train. My father worked for the New York and Long Branch Railroad, and naturally, we rode on passes. Mama was just the lady to make good use of that, and after a hot day trotting around New York, we always had a nice cool sail home on the *Sandy Hook*, but how I hated that boat train! It stopped at everybody's back yard. I don't know how they got up a head of steam to start up between those short stretches between so many stations.

—Elizabeth S. Smith

ROUTE 36 OR NAVESINK AVENUE

Before Route 36 became a four-lane highway, before the trolley came and the trolley went, it was a two-lane dirt road. Just beyond our place, as it started to curve toward Atlantic Highlands, it formed a rather steep hill from 254 Navesink Avenue to Water Witch Avenue. This often caused trouble.

At least once every summer, a heavily laden wagon would travel down the hill a bit faster than the horses. This would cause the wagon to bump the horses, spooking them to run away. When the pounding hooves of the run away horses sounded through the neighborhood, doors flew open all along the block as men poured forth to chase and catch the horses. They were caught within a short distance, much to the relief of the frightened driver.

Later, when the trolley came it was a different story. Sometimes the trolley came gliding down the hill only to have the pole leave the overhead wire when it reached the foot of the hill. Sparks flew all over, and the trolley slowed to a stop. The motorman jumped down, hauled the pole back in place and the trolley went on its way. It was very exciting.

—Ann McNeill

Under Twin Lights

For the benefit of those persons who have never gone out of the river by boat, particularly under sail, there is something very comforting, I feel, about coming into the river under Twin Lights.

It really doesn't matter whether your trip was around the world or just out into the ocean on a summer day for a cruise. Outside the water is choppy and sometimes downright rough. Your boat rocks and pitches. If the wind is light, the rigging jerks and slats; if it is breezy, the spray flies. The racket sometimes obliges conversation to be shouted. It is exciting and great fun in good weather.

As you come under the seemingly watchful eyes of the Twin Lights, your ears are startled by the sudden quiet and the smooth water deceived your legs, which are still attuned to the pitching of the deck. Gradually you become aware of the gentle gurgle of the bow wave.

You have come home to the familiar and protected waters of the Shrewsbury River, as have so many before.

—June Methot
1966

This steel engraving by renowned artist Granville Perkins was included in the 1872 publication *Picturesque America*. "The Highlands of the Navesink have the post of honor among the American hills." The original watercolor rendition is on display at the Twin Lights museum.

THE BRIDGE

Fond memories still remain of the old railroad drawbridge. Starting at the foot of East View Hill, it joined Highlands with Sandy Hook. It was an all-purpose bridge. It had a footpath, a road for vehicles and railroad tracks. The tracks extended more than half way across the river where they veered to the right on a trestle leading to Sea Bright.

The beauty of the bridge was that it turned. Whenever a boat wanted to pass through, it tooted and the bridge tooted back. If we were lucky enough to be near the bridge when that happened, we ran like crazy to get on the bridge and get a ride as it swung open. It turned slowly, and the boat went sliding past so very carefully. The boat was so near that we could call back and forth to the people on board. Then the bridge turned slowly back into place, and we had two rides for free.

—Ann McNeill

The Highlands Drawbridge

In the fast paced world we live in today, when we can reach just about anyplace in the world as quickly as we can dial a phone or click "send" for e-mail, we have no patience for the opening of the Highlands–Sea Bright bridge. What a pain it is! A little boat has to hold up all this traffic? Doesn't the owner know that I am in a hurry? But there was a time years ago when people did not feel this way.

We used to have a house in Belmar when I was little. About fifty years ago, before they built the Parkway, going down there in the summer must have been more complicated for my family than it was in olden days for people going West in wagon trains. Even though we had the house, we didn't go until after the Fourth of July, because it seemed to take us so much time just to think and plan about it. We had to pack up the old Plymouth. Then it was an all-day trip from home. We would get an early start, and then my father would groan that he just couldn't stand to confront this terrible drive from

The fourth Highlands-Sea Bright drawbridge, built in 1932, was called the "Million Dollar Bridge" for its cost and its beautiful design. For area kids, jumping from the Sea Bright side into the river was something of a right of passage. For most motorists, it was a downright nuisance when open, now alleviated by today's fifth bridge. The Sandlass House, the last remnant of Highland Beach, is seen at left of bridge.

Hillside where we lived. About sixty miles, I guess, to Belmar from Hillside. And we would just turn around and go back! And be very disappointed.

But the bridge was the midway point. The excitement, the thing that kept us going was wondering "Would that bridge be up?" It seemed like it was one of the Seven Wonders of the World to us. And we would watch and watch to see. "Yes, it's up!" And we would just marvel how this great big bridge would go up into the air. All the traffic had to stop, and if we were really lucky, we'd be on the bridge when the draw went up, and the road turned magically into something else. It wasn't a road anymore. You could get out in the middle of the road and stand in the middle of the highway. All the other people were getting out of their cars also, and we could go over to the edge of the bridge and look down. You didn't have to stay in your car and there wasn't any policeman to tell you it wasn't safe, wasn't allowed. This was so wonderful to me. You could see this wonderful little town and all the river and the boats on it. It was like looking at Brigadoon. It was this enchanted little town, tucked away by the side there and under the bridge. And then, too soon, we would marvel at how the bridge came down. Everyone would get back into their cars, and this little observation place turned back into a road again. The excitement was over. My father would groan again, and off we would go toward Belmar.

—Maya Walsh

I Come to Highlands

I first arrived in Highlands with a tenant who lived in my mother's house. Mrs. Marthens this the lady was. I came here for the summer, that summer to help her because she had been ill. She was Mrs. Nellie Marthens. And this lady lived up at the end of the old railroad which is now Shore Drive. Her house went straight across Locust and Willow Streets, and she had a bungalow there. That was, oh, God, I guess that was 1929, and I came to help her. They used to have of a lot of men who came down to go fishing, and in addition I used to park the cars in addition to helping her. Now Roy Maxson was the iceman, and he delivered to her, and she had about four or five bungalows she owned, and he delivered to them. That's how I met him, and he was real charming and he looked just like Errol Flynn and he had a real line, which, you know, at that time, me to the stupid kid. That was in June that I first met him, and later when I went back to the city, he came up to see me and all. Well, we got married that November. The sixth, 1930, I think.

Then I came to Highlands to live and it was the greatest shock of my life because I came from a house, from a house in Brooklyn down to well life in, you know, Highlands. What a shock for a young city girl from a house in Brooklyn.

—Lillian Maxson
From an interview by grandson David Maxson, 1996

The Railroad Brought Me Here

I came back from service in 1946. I had my opportunity by seniority to take the jobs that had come open during the war. We had a very fine gentleman who was mayor of Highlands, George Hardy. He was also the agent at the Highlands Station. Right after the war was over, he retired and they had a young man working the job who was not a telegrapher, and they still handled the Western Union messages and he said, "Well, that's a good job." And that's how I got to Highlands. I was there for a while and as things progressed I worked at different places along the Seashore Branch of the Jersey Central. I went to Atlantic Highlands, Port Monmouth, and because I was a telegrapher, I became a train dispatcher at Long Branch in 1949. I liked Highlands. We live right below the Twin Lights, just under where the Postal Telegraph had a marine telegraph station back before the days of radio.

—G. Lester Whitfield

Operation Sail

We're aboard the *Jakbar* on this historic occasion. Tall sailing ships from countries around the world here helping us celebrate America's 200th Birthday!

Sandy Hook Bay and the Inner Harbor are filled with these magnificent old sailing ships all getting ready for the grand parade of ships up the Hudson River. What a magnificent sight. This must have been what it was like when our grandfather worked aboard great sailing ships like these. I guess salt

USCGC *Eagle* led the fleet sailing ships from around the world in Op Sail '76 to celebrate the 200th Anniversary of U.S. Independence.

water's been in our blood all this time. Our dad was a marine and here we still are with Bahrs Landing right on the river.

We are passing the *San Sebastian*, a Spanish ship. All around the crew is all dolled-up and dressed-up in their bright white outfits. They're in the rigging too, on the yard arms. All its signal flags are flying for decoration. This is very exciting.

Just passed a German ship, they too all in uniform and everyone is hollering to us in the little boats passing, "Vie Gehts?" A beautiful, beautiful sight.

Hello, we're now passing the *Liberdad* from Argentina and all the sailors and crew are dressed in white pants, blue and white striped top and bolero hats. The yard arms are polished, they're bright, colorful flags flying in the good breeze. This is a great trip. The ship as we pass it on our starboard, they're just unfurling the sails. The men are up on the top yard arms standing on the foot ropes and letting the huge white sails spill down. The sails are standing out in the little breeze blowing. Look, there's an American flag on the top mast! How I'd like to take a cruise on that vessel. If I was younger… Well, I don't think I'll live to see a sight like this, magnificent, thrilling, ever again in my lifetime. God bless America!

—John A. Bahrs, July 4, 1976

Part 3

Clamming, the Heart of Highlands

On the River

I first started clammin' when I was about seven years old. I was out there when I was seven. My dad used to take me out clammin' all the time. He taught me how to clam. Used to catch fifteen bushels, easily, anywhere. After the Army, at about twenty, I started clammin' seriously. It's only basically pullin' the hoe up and down, you know. It doesn't take no great intelligence to pull a hoe up and down, but in the long run it does. Take a person never soft clammed before and you put that hoe in their hand. I seen everybody do it. They break it, bend it or break all the clams. You know, there's an education to that, see. Soft clammin', churnin' with a hoe, is gonna be a lost art. I know where there's big beds of soft clams nobody ever touched. You know what they're usin'? A little bitta rake, like you use in the garden, getting' on their knee and diggin' 'em. I'm sayin' to myself, "Why don't they use a churnin' hoe?"

The Indians were basically the first clammers. Then there was a man on the hill a long time ago and he used to play around with the Indians. He's the one started soft clammin' and hard clammin.' Don't know for sure his name, but he used to live up there on the hill.

Clammin' isn't like a job. You can be serious about it one year and not serious the next. You have the opportunity of goin' out and bein' rich or stayin' home. So, sometimes I'd decide to be rich, I'd go out. Sometimes I wouldn't go out and be poor.

I don't know about any others, but for this man, it becomes very habit formin', addictin', workin' on the river. You couldn't ask for a better life than workin' on the river. That's the best life a man can have.

—Wendi Matthews, from an interview by Richard Maxson Jr.

CLAMMING STORIES

When I first got married and arrived in Highlands, I never thought I was going to do the things I had to do. My husband, Roy, was a clammer, and his father, Burt Maxson, before him was a clammer. That wasn't his main job, but when times were hard, Burt went clamming. He grew up in Highlands and in Locust Point, up near Locust bridge—that's where he originally was from—and then he came to Highlands and raised his family here. Roy was his son, and Roy went clamming and so did Pop.

But Pop...I don't know if I should say this. In those days, when a clammer went clamming, he brought home his catch, and he didn't have no middleman: he had his own customers. These customers he delivered to faithfully, you know. And at that time, you only got 50¢ a bushel, and you had to work hard. The winters were hard, and you had to work off the ice. They drew their clams across the river on sleds. Well, poor Pop, his customers

Three of the many Highlands soft-clam shucking and packing shanties that used to dot the shore, here circa 1910.

never got their clams because Pop would take them to some tavern, and he would take it out in trade. He would drink all the profits. Beer was 5¢ a glass, and he only got 50¢ a bushel. And he drank up the clams. Then he would drive his old truck home. How he ever drove home, I don't know.

My life as the wife of a clammer, which I didn't very well like in the beginning. My husband would go clamming and bring home the clams. And I would have to open the clams til my fingers were, oh, terrible, all cut up, you know how they get. And then I had to wash off the clams, and I had to soak them overnight. The next day, I put them in quart jars, and Roy and I delivered them, and we had many customers over in Fair Haven and Rumson. And after all this work of the getting the clams on the river and me opening them and all, we got the huge sum of the 25¢ a quart.

Now today I don't know why I did it, but I did it because it was a livelihood and extra money, and sometimes it was the only money. And that's where John Azzolina would come in and give us credit. That was the way we lived.

All this time I had to sit and open the clams, I had to sit in front of a stove, which had to have wood fed into it constantly, which to me, that was a funny thing. I lived at 80 Miller Street. I opened the clams in the kitchen, in front of the wood stove.

—Lillian Maxson, from an interview by David Maxson, 1996

Clam Shanties

Many of the ladies in the town were widowed, or they worked to help their husbands, and so on. They had what they called "clam shanties." I remember them down at the foot of Miller Street. The women would get up and be at the dock from 4 a.m. opening clams. They would have a potbelly stove for heat, and many of them had a wonderful sense of humor. They were joking and laughing, even though this was a difficult job. Their poor hands were cut and scraped, and they would still open clams. As I recall, my friend Vera Fong's mother worked in the clam shanty. We used to go down there, and they would put as many clams on each finger as they could hold. Then they would fill a quart jar, and the clams would be packed in ice. Their husbands, or the men who owned the clamming business, would take them up to the city, mostly New York, to the Fulton Fish Market. That was a daily procedure.

—Mae Bahrs

Shucking Clams

I began opening clams when I was sixteen years old in the mid-1920s, and did it for eighteen years. The fishermen used to bring the baskets of clams into our shanty. There was room inside to store them. On cold days, the men culled the clams in that room into two sizes, those to be opened and those to be sold as steamers. We had competitions amongst us as we opened. We'd get jealous if one of the girls got much ahead of the rest of us. Each of us wanted to get the largest clams because they were the easiest to open, so we'd make more money. The sizes of the clams which came in was according to the tide. If there was a big tide off, the fishermen got bigger clams. Sometimes, in the winter when the men dug through the ice, the clams we opened had ice in them.

They were hard days. We worked so hard, and it was tiresome, but we had fun while we opened. Somebody'd say something foolish, and we'd all laugh. Our backs would be killing us by the time we quit. Sometimes, a man would come down to our shanty and play a guitar and sing to us. Somebody else might bring a pie or some buns and coffee. We went home for lunch. Our homes were nearby.

Lent was a heavy demand time for soft clams, when the Catholics couldn't eat meat. We worked long hours then. Sometimes during Lent, we'd finish up in one shanty and go to work in another.

—Margaret Worth Kendrick
From an interview on October 18, 1985, by Clyde L. MacKenzie

Clam Buyers

My father had the business before me. He started in business in 1912 by floating the clams he dug and selling them to a large restaurant. Then he began buying from other clammers. That's the way all small businesses got started. I began clamming in the summer when I was twelve years old and sold to my father. When I was thirteen, I worked all summer clamming. When I was fourteen, I left school and was a full-time clammer thereafter. I had no further education. When my father retired, I took over the business.

About ten clammers used to sell to us in the summer, maybe five or six in the winter. We had one hired man who helped put the clams in and out of trays. We sold a lot of clams to Lundy Brothers in Sheepshead Bay on

Coney Island. Every day during the summer, they sent a truck over and picked up thirty to fifty bushels. In the winter, it would be three times a week. Lundy's redistributed some of the clams over in Sheepshead Bay to various restaurants. We also sold to clam bars in Atlantic City. I ran the clam business for twenty-five to thirty years.

—Chris Kohlenbusch
From an interview on June 16, 1986, by Clyde L. MacKenzie

Treading Clams

We treaded when the water got warm. We put our feet close together and parallel, then twisted them as we moved sideward to feel the clams. We picked them up with our hands. There was no rake going that'll catch clams as fast as hands can. Treading was tough on the feet, as it tore them up, and there was no way to avoid it. We used mostly the heel of our feet because that's the hardest part, not our toes because shells in the bottom would cut them off. When we first began in the summer, we felt like we were walking on eggs as

Watermen in 1946, with the railroad station in the background. *Upper row, left to right:* Wallace Hartsgrove, Gilbert Layton, Herbert Hartsgrove, Don Hodson, Vince Worth; *lower:* George Mount, Elmer Layton. Identified by Leslie Layton.

we walked down the street. By the end of summer, our legs felt a foot shorter. The best treading was in water about knee-deep. There were fellas here who would catch one thousand to two thousand clams in two hours.

—Jimmy White
From an interview on July 15, 1989, by Clyde L. MacKenzie

Clammer in the Slammer

My name is David Maxson and I am writing this story sitting in my cell at the Monmouth County Correctional Institution in Freehold. I received a six month jail sentence for harvesting shellfish from specially restricted waters of the Shrewsbury River. This is the second time I have been incarcerated for illegal clamming and my fourth offense overall. Three of those four were planned acts of bootlegging, the local term for digging and selling clams illegally.

I was born and raised in Highlands, traditionally a clam digger town and I have been bootlegging clams from the Shrewsbury and Navesink rivers sporadically since I was about twelve years old.

I sold my first illegal clams for five cents apiece. A little later on I can remember going out clamming evenings with a local bootlegger family which included the father (who drove the station wagon and dropped us off and picked us up with our catch), all the siblings, a few cousins, a couple of friends and myself. Even the mother had a part: it as her job to insure a sufficient supply of red onion sacks used for transporting our illicit product, and to have plenty of hot coffee and hot chocolate waiting for us when we returned home. Then we would all gather to count the clams and determine out pay for the evening. It was, literally, a family affair.

Of course, even at that young age, I was quite aware of the illegality of what we were doing. But between eight and twelve years old, back then in the early seventies, earning ten to twenty dollars a trip and having a good time doing it, I tended to overlook the fact that I was breaking the law.

Everybody, it seemed, was doing it, parents and children alike. And when we sold our clams to respectable people in the community, all of whom knew, of course, that they were purchasing bootleg clams, it only served to reinforce my belief that basically I was doing nothing wrong.

I continued my bootlegging habits for several years, stopping when I was about fifteen, when I began legal soft clamming. Steamers were plentiful then and I was making good money so there was no reason for me to bootleg. Things went along fairly well for the next seven or eight years, until, for still unexplained reasons, the soft clams virtually disappeared. Initially this was not a problem for me, because a few years earlier the state had approved a depuration plant for hard shell clams similar to the ones which had been used to purify soft clams. Simply put, it's a state regulated system that transforms polluted clams into non-polluted edible product, soaking it in a tank of continuously circulating and processed water for 48 hours.

I switched back to hard clamming, legally this time. The money was still good, but not nearly as good as when I was soft clamming. Knowing that I could get a higher fairer price by selling my clams directly to the bootleg middleman, or an even better price selling directly to fish markets and restaurants. So I went back to bootlegging.

A common practice would be to dig, say six bushels, hide three of them, sell three to the plant as a legal catch, and return at night to retrieve the hidden clams to be sold at perhaps double the plant price. It was a prevalent practice, engaged in by many besides myself.

I truly believe that had such a large bite not been taken out by the depuration process, the practice of bootlegging would have been reduced to practically nil. I remember one summer being promised, week after week, that the price we were receiving for our legal clams would be going up a semi-respectable 12 or 13 cents apiece, only to pull away from the dock disappointed after learning the price remained at 8 to 10 cents. This would take the heart out of me, as my late grandfather, Roy Maxson, also a clammer, used to say, and I would begin formulating a plan to successfully bootleg some of my catch for the day.

I did this until I got caught for the third time. That's when I received a 90 day jail sentence and served 21 days. This taught me a lesson. I stopped my illegal activities and began clamming legally, until the plant closed down through mismanagement. I found myself entirely out of work.

I had a choice this time: either quit clamming, a pursuit I followed since childhood and loved, or make an attempt to switch to the relay program. That required that clams dug in local (polluted) be transported or relayed to cleaner, unrestricted waters farther south in Barnegat Bay. Mainly it required pretty much double the work of normal clamming. Usually, a clam is dug and sold locally. With the relay program, a clam must be dug, loaded into a state approved truck, driven south, loaded into another boat and taken out

Bill and Joe Kendrick, like all Highlands clammers, took no winter vacation from harvesting clams, at times cutting river ice and raking clams in frigid water. It's a tough and sometimes dangerous occupation, but one not to be traded for any other job.

to a leased lot, dumped onto the bottom, and re-dug 30 or more days later, carried back north and sold.

Finding this intolerable, I began bootlegging again, having no other means to make a living. Needless to say, that's what landed me again in the hoosegow, enjoying the company of people who have done a bit worse than dig some allegedly polluted clams.

—David Maxson

Part 4

Summer Vacation

Fond Memories of a Gravelly Childhood

Nobody I know had a better time as a kid than I did. Each spring, before the city streets of northern New Jersey got too hot, my parents took my sister Nancy and me to the Jersey Shore. As we drove down Routes 1 and 9, then Route 35, the annual trip to the Highlands seemed endless. Though we were only going to open up the bungalow for the season, we knew that the few remaining weeks of school would drag before we spent three glorious months swimming in the Navesink, getting dirty on Red Clay Hill, and spying on the "rival" kids at Conners.

What memories! The big trains behind Mulligan's bringing the fathers from New York and other cities up north where they worked. Putting pennies on the tracks so they'd be smashed as big as fifty cent pieces. Flood high tides in the mornings where we played ring-o-lereo from the slide and the pier. Kicking up "super suds" on the two old life rafts. My father and I digging cherry stone clams in the shallow water when he came down Friday evenings. My Mother and Grandmother sitting in the same spot on the beach for years and years. Did all the mothers lease their spots? Buying lunches of hot dogs, sodas, and Cracker Jacks from Conners Canteen and sneaking looks at the older Connors girls dancing to the jukebox.

For me, the other kids were the best part. In my pre-teen years, it seemed like half of Brooklyn came to the Shore. The Mikes (Flood and

Gravelly Point bungalows are shown to the left and right of the row of trees, in the late 1920s. Conners's bungalows are to the left, creating a tight knit social summer community.

Quaid), Paul Carberry, and I were a team. We always let that athletic kid from the Bronx, Billy Klika, play with us even though he wasn't strictly from Gravelly. Throw in the Bremerkamps from Hoboken, Paul's brother Ed, and a few assorted others, and we could always get a baseball game together in a moments notice.

But, baseball wasn't our only recreation. As we got older, we discovered girls. As the Good Humor Man's appearance after dinner lost its appeal, we looked forward to late night beachfires. Sally O'Hara from Roxy's and Carol Kennedy from Conners suddenly became friends. Nights on the pier with cases of Schaefer, Mike Flood singing Buddy Holly songs on his guitar, and the rest of us singing along or drifting off in couples were surely among the highlights of my adolescence. Then there was painting Buoy Number 8, Bungalow Day races and parties, movies in the old summer house, hanging out in the park across from the Old Lady's store, and Saturday nights at the movies in town.

There were others whom I'll never forget. Mr. and Mrs. Giles, whose stern presence kept order! Uncle Billy with his big drum leading the ragamuffins parade on Bungalow Day. Johnny Gardner who taught me to swim. Clyde Wolff who taught me about fluke fishing in his aluminum boat. Audrey and Walter Bluhm taking me with them to Red Bank for ice cream before they were married. Johnny Gay and Dennis Redmond, the big guys I thought were cool. Mrs. Mahoney who cared about all of us, and later wrote to me while I was on my government paid trip to the Far East.

I think back often and fondly on my thirteen years at Gravelly. As the years go by I realize how much of what I am comes from those days. My love for salt water, boating and fishing, beach parties, and an appreciation of different kinds of people, all come from Gravelly Point.

—Rick Geffken
August 1989

Highlands' Golden Era

I am Edna Kruse and I live at 16 Bay Ave. I used to run the popular tavern called Captain's Corner. I have lived in Highlands practically all my life. I love it and nowadays one of favorite things is to relive the old times through photographs, mementos and my memory of Highlands in its Golden Days.

My family moved here to Highlands in 1902 from New York City. It seems to me that people had a lot more enthusiasm then, for simple things, too. I remember when my family, the McGuires, had a telephone put in our restaurant, the McGuire House, on what is now the Bahrs Landing site—Jack Bahrs bought the place in 1917. It must have been the first telephone in the borough and it caused such a stir. Folks would look for pretexts to use it and they felt so important when they got a call. I often had to walk over the old Shrewsbury bridge to deliver messages, but being a youngster, I never gave the long trek a thought.

I remember many famous figures of the late 1890s and early years of this century. I would hear grown ups talking about visiting actress Lily Langtry, the Blonde Venus; Diamond Jim Brady, with his jeweled waistcoat; matinee idol Lillian Russell and her big appetite for ears of corn; Col. Jim Fisk's yacht rounding Sandy Hook with its many singing canaries and liveried crew. Of course these were Olympian figures for me, only seen at a distance.

Summer visitors swarmed to the Highlands area in the years following the turn of the century. The sands here and there frequently resembled army camps. Folks would rent a summer tent for $25 and get their water from a pump attached to a pipe sunk deep into the ground. Even the well-to-do staying at the east View House were casual about swim suits; they would just roll up skirts and trousers and go into the water. Their favorite past-times were berry picking, in the Twin Lights Woods, horse back and carriage riding, hiking, all while snugly dressed from head to toe with no concession made for the summer heat.

Wallace Reid, later to become the World War One movie star, lived in the Highlands, in the hills. His mother indulged him and he received the first automobile in the borough. When he took my sister and me for a ride it was like a dream flight to us. You had to climb three steps to enter the car. I recall Wally was a good natured boy, always happiest when someone was enjoying things with him.

One of my actual guests was Sir Thomas Lipton. His *Shamrock* lost the America's Cup races many times here off Sandy Hook. The races brought people from everywhere, of course. Places on Mt. Michill's scenic drive, the highest point on the Atlantic coast, were at a premium, and so were seats on borough roof tops. When the winner rounded the Hook, I guess we went a little wild. Sir Thomas Lipton would stop at our hotel for a cup of cheer. He was a tall, tanned, with steel-grey hair, laugh-easy gentleman with a sly sense of humor. A pleasure to talk to, honestly kind.

Here's one of the old daily advertisements we typed and put on every summer bungalow door and at the hotels.

> *KRUSE'S PAVILLION, Highlands, New Jersey.*
> *SUNDAY EVENING—AUGUST 7: DON'T FORGET OLD TIMERS NIGHT THIS EVENING.*
> *After the Ball is Over; Carry Me Back to Old Virginia; School Days; Come Back to Erin; Just a Song at Twilight.*
> *GET THE HABIT—DANCE EVERY EVENING—IT'S HEALTHFUL EXERCISE. GO TO KRUSE'S PAVILLION THAT'S WHERE THE CROWDS GO.*

—Edna Kruse

First Impressions

Well, I was a very small child [when first in Highlands] and it reminded me of a western town. Bay Ave. was a gravel road, and there were hotels all along. One in particular was Johnson's Hotel, right on the corner of Bay Ave. and Miller St. That had rocking chairs, and it just looked like something you would see in a western town.

My mother married Randolph Borden, who was a wonderful man. He had a business at 50 Miller St; he had a soda fountain, candy store, ice cream parlor, and luncheonette and pool parlor.

—Mae Bahrs

Flashbacks from Florida

My mother and father, Mr. and Mrs. Mahoney, who lived in what they often called the "wooden tent" at 68 Gravelly Point, all summer long, sang a song called "Memories, Memories, Dreams of Long Ago" and so from a vantage point of my late sixties, I spin for you my Memories.

Water Witch, Gravelly Point, Conners, Roxy's, Bay street, train station, Sandy Hook, the Red Hill, trees and a bumpy road, friends who were like family—the extended family of Gravelly and its summer are part of my early years. From a sea of memories it isn't easy to pick out that which stands out. All of it is part of the collage of my life.

Come the spring of every year, we started counting the days. My sisters, Edith and Gert, and I watched as days passed, grew more pleasant and became Gravelly Days. Come Decoration Day, now called Memorial Day,

Tent camping, as shown here at Gravelly Point, was the rule for summer visitors to Highlands, with more than a dozen sites with tents known in 1910. All these gradually were upgraded to cottages (later year-round residences), as at Gravelly Point.

we just had to go and check it out. There it was, our "wooden tent," all boarded up against the harshness of winter. It was waiting there to be undressed and brought to life again.

And so it was by the end of June, the awesome job of "getting out the first dirt" began. Unscrambling the jungle of stuff which was stored against the high winds of winter, the four beavers toiled. What seemed like an eternity was only a couple of days. Sixty-eight was ready to go! Spic and Span were the bywords as we swept, scrubbed, dusted, ironed, hung, and happily worked to make it recover from its winter sleep.

The day school closed we bounced from the classrooms and made the long drive, an all day affair from the streets of New York to the sands, sun, and water of Gravelly. A dirt road with lots of holes which were to fill up with rain and tree-lined to form an arch over the Lotus Land led to number 68 and the edge of the water. We jumped out of the car and ran to the beach. It was still there! We gaped at the pier with a raft at the end, the summer house, the rowboats at the mooring, and on and on—our first review of our summer place.

On to its people! Who's down? Who's coming? The Wests, the Jablonskis, the Webers, the Scanlons, the Moores, the Beyers, the Floods. All of these people appear in my collage.

It was simple fun, sand, water, canoes, boats, and baseball, wiener roasts, digging clams, and just wandering about with friends. I grew up with Gravelly's family.

In those days supermarkets were not on every corner and if available were at a distance. Cars being not so prevalent, groceries came to us. The bakery truck, the fruit and vegetable truck, the milk truck, the iceman, and without fail, the Good Humor truck. I can still see and taste the crumb cake!

We dug lots of clams and most every family had a pitchfork. Those now expensive steamed clams of today were the lowly clams of yesterday's baskets under a lot of bungalows. Periodically my mother would yell, "Get rid of those clams!," which in a day or two smelled up the entire house.

My memories see my father, Joe Jablonski, Freddie Beyer, and Johnnie Moore trying to unload the enormous catches of fluke, porgies, bluefish, and weakfish. Few wanted them. Our fishermen only caught fish; they didn't clean the fish, so it was an "as is" a situation.

Lobsters and lobster boats are forever a memory. Every morning out they went. Traps piled high in the boat center. The lobsterman sometimes in a rain slicker looking just like the famous New England fisherman. A steady

Left: Rob Cottrell taking lobsters and assorted nonedible creatures from a lobster pot and re-baiting it with cod or haddock.

Below: Conners Cedar Grove hotel and cottages, circa 1925. William H. Conners turned swampland into one of the shore's best-known and loved summer resorts. All of the resort has disappeared, except one cottage used as an office for the apartments and condos, to make space for parking for Seastreak commuters on boats to New York.

stream every morning and a reverse in the evening. We ate mountains of lobsters. I think we ate the lobstermen out of business

We lived in the water. All of us had three or four bathing suits. Barefooted we went for weeks on end, until shoes became the torture for Sunday mass. As the sun went down, we went home, showered and dressed because it was time for the commuters. The *Sandy Hook* and the *Mary Patten* could be seen pulling in and the Jersey Central as it came down the tracks to Water Witch station. Hot tired, overdressed fathers stepped off and all of us straggled with them down our road. We always went swimming again with father. I wonder now why we dressed up to meet the train since most of us went right back in the water with our fathers.

At the top of their road, close by, was Mulligan's—mostly a beer place, but later groceries also. For a good long time Mulligan's had a slated board porch. When we realized that people dropped coins through the slats we took to crawling in the space beneath and retrieving of the coins. We never even talked about it. This was clandestine activity.

Periodically we had northeast storms. Days and days of wind, rain and muddy roads, wet shoes, wet clothes, and we used to wander about soaking wet and sweatered, yet between the squalls we played endless games of monopoly, cards, made model airplanes out of balsa wood—no such thing as plastics back then. We also complained, argued, and felt deprived.

The trouble with turning on memories is the difficulty you have in turning them off. Believe me the Florida coast on which I have lived for almost 35 years was never like Gravelly. It just doesn't have the heart. My love, and thanks for the memories!

—Marge Mahoney Ballinger

Conners Hotel

I recall Conners being the most attractive and prominent summer gathering place in Highlands. It was then called Conners Cedar Grove Hotel. There were tall, mature cedar trees scattered throughout the property. The hotel with its spacious porch filled with rocking chairs, the classy attire of the guests, and the well kept facilities and grounds conveyed a sense of simple refinement, splendor and elegance.

There was a row of rental bungalows, all identical, along each side of the property from the railroad to the river. From the Carriage House to the hotel was a walkway covered by a rustic cedar bower on which grew grape vines. There were several benches built in it which were very popular with couples at night. The large stucco building was the owners' residence. My sister tells me that in the early teens they raised pigs up near the railroad. The entire area from the railroad to the river was neatly kept lawns, flower and vegetable gardens and a neat gravel driveway.

Across the railroad was a sandlot baseball field, used on weekends by the many people attending picnics, clambakes, etc. at the hotel. During the week we kids used it for games.

There was dancing every evening in the hotel to the music of a 3–4 piece live band. We kids watched through the windows.

Every summer large groups from the city came to Conners for picnics and clambakes. One large excursion boat that frequently came was the *Pan America*. By the time the boat left in the evening some of the passengers needed help to get aboard. There was never a lack of empty whiskey bottles in the garbage behind the hotel, notwithstanding the 18th amendment of Prohibition.

I am indeed fortunate that my memories of Conners Hotel are from when it was at the peak of its splendor and popularity.

—Robert Herpich

Summer Fun for Five Generations

I remember waking up for another long wonderful day on our beach.

Our porch is where my Mom and Dad [Mae and John Flood] and us used to sit and discuss all our thoughts. My father used to know everyone. He'd call to Mazie and Alberta, Mrs. Mahoney and Ted Dick next door. They used to discuss all the woes and wonders of the world.

None of the kids changed clothes the way kids do now, two and three times a day. We spent our whole day playing spud on the beach and tag under the boats. If we saw someone, we would just go under and tag them. I guess now as adults, we wouldn't care too much for that game.

We played hide-and-seek until we went in at night. We went on hikes to Henry Hudson Spring. We rode our bikes to the Old Lady's (where the Parrot is now) for ice cream and walked to the Post Office every day to see if our boy friends wrote to us and stopped at Johnnie's candy store for a coke on the way back.

We had nothing but fun. We thought it boring but when the end of the summer came we would all cry and take the train home, dog and all.

I remember the Bungalow Day races always being held on the road. Mary Jane Scanlon and Carol Quaid were really great runners and I always won the Japanese Crab race (so did my brother John Flood, Mike Flood and Mike Quaid).

My father told us of Picnics they used to have on Sandy Hook. Everyone got into their rowboats and off they went, kids, Mom and Dad, food and drink (imagine the return trip home).

The slide was really the best. We had long trains of kids going down. We went down sidewards, backwards and rear-end first. Our slide had a wonderful bump in the middle. What a ball!

There have been five generations living in #73: my grandparents, my Mom and Dad, my sister, Mary Patane, John and Mike Flood, our children Anne Marie Frescia, Eileen Sherank, Jimmy, Regina and Danny Byrnes and our newest addition, little Tommy.

We love it, always have, and always will.

—Anne Byrnes, August 1989

Best of Life at Conners

My Dad (Joseph Conlon) was brought to Conners when he was six months old, in June, 1896. The bungalows weren't built then and they had a tent. Dad brought mother (Theresa Conlon) when they were engaged, 1921, I think, and after they married, they had the bungalow (#27) next door to Grandma and Grandpa Conlon (#26). The bungalow was furnished with a table and chairs, beds, an indoor bathroom and an outdoor shower. We had an extra bedroom added, which gave us four bedrooms. We supplied our own linens, pots and pans, and dishes.

Food shopping was done right there in the town of Highlands. There was an A&P, Cotton Market, Ralph the Shoemaker, Fehlhaber the tailor and cleaner. It was very complete shopping at the time.

Dad commuted all week from New York. He took the Sandy Hook boat to the Atlantic Highlands pier. The train met the boat and continued south as far as Long Branch or possibly further. He would get off at Water Witch station, which is now a bank.

Dad knew Marie Conners as a child growing up. Also when she married Herman Black and had the four Black boys, Bill, Duke, Jack, and Bob, until she died in 1948.

They had a very exclusive club, the Canasta Club. They played cards every week and took turns entertaining in each others' bungalows. They enjoyed each others' company and always had a good time. Dues were collected each week and by the end of the season they had enough money for a big dinner out. They dropped in at a few places on the Sea Bright strip. But they always ended up at Conners who always treated them royally.

Towards the end of summer they celebrated Bungalow Day. Everyone decorated their bungalows in various themes. During the day there were races, swimming, diving, running, wheelbarrow, three-legged; there was always a big baseball game. At night there was a big dinner and dancing for the grown ups—we teenagers ate hotdogs and hamburgers and hung out at the stand on the beach.

Conners was a special place and I don't think it could ever be duplicated in today's world. It was family oriented and out of it came great friendships and even romances and marriages. We had the best of life at Conners.

—Theresa Conlon, 1996

What a Bustling Resort!

Highlands was some busy, bustling resort. It's hard to believe it today. Bay Ave. back then was the main buy and sell thoroughfare, a boulevard of fun when the summer crowds arrived. Frequently it saw thousands of people milling about, buying ice cream, sodas, hot dogs, and crab sandwiches. Several wheel games were present, along with other innumerable games

The Highlands merry-go-round, shown here in the aftermath of an autumn hurricane. This landmark, still in the fun-filled memories of many Highlanders, was destroyed in a huge blaze on February 19, 1964.

of skill. And the merry-go-round! Highlands had swinging doors and slot machines, huge 5 cent mugs of beer and singing waiters. Some visitors stayed the whole summer, some just a week or a couple of days. Some came on the five steamboats and some on the 90 trains of the Jersey Central for just a single day of fun in Highlands.

—Edna Kruse

The Dance Hall

On Bay Ave. just a few hundred feet north of Bahrs there was a dance hall owned and operated by Barney Creighton. It really wasn't on Bay Ave., but was built on the river bank and extended out over the river.

On the right side of the grounds leading to the hall there was a row of small stands where snacks and souvenirs were sold. The Dance Hall itself was enclosed in glass which gave the dancers a beautiful view of the river. At nights the lights from the building shone across the water. The front wall was about four feet high; not too high for us children to press our noses against the glass and watch the dancers glide around the floor.

Of course, we dreamed of the day when we too would be big enough to join the dancers. After some time it became Kruse's Dance Hall. After that it vanished and only memories were left.

—Ann McNeill

Beaches

In the early days of Highlands many of the beaches were privately owned. Conners, Neimark's and the beaches along Fifth St. Neimark's was a large beach across from Bay Ave where Harry Neimark had his garage and bungalows. It became a marina and lots of condos are built there now. On one of the beaches on Valley St. [actually Cedar St.] gold was discovered. What a wild and wonderful time that was! Miller St. beach was the best. It had a pavilion, water fountains, bath houses and showers. There was a bulkhead you could walk on to the diving board and the swimming area was roped in. Leslie Layton and Wallace Parker were lifeguards there. There was also a float and a slide. The water was so clear you could see bottom. We caught killies, and horseshoe crabs and popped bubble grass (dried seaweed). We wet the stems of seagrass and wrote on our legs, then poured sand on it. We would lay in the sun and after a few hours brush off the sand and there was our "tattoo." A typical summer day meant walking up to Roxy's and jumping off the dock as the tide was coming in. We floated to Neimark's, then to Miller St. beach and finally to the Bridge beach. Lots of kids dove off the bridge and they also had a cable swing out over the water.

—Mae Rugg

They All Looked Happy

I look at pictures of those families in your book [*The Highlands, Images of America*], sitting in front of those tents or those cottages that were almost in the water, neither of which had bathrooms and yet they all looked happy and as if they were having fun. I was always finicky from a little kid on and all I could see in those pictures were the damp beds and clothes, the mildew smell especially during a long rainy spell! That would be the worst. Along with all that I remember the mosquitoes, gnats and those horrible black flies that showed up on the beaches when there was

Two carousels or merry-go-rounds entertained visitors and residents in the early 1900s: the one shown here on Highlands Beach and, a short walk across the bridge, the one in Highlands on Bay Avenue.

no air stirring and could they ever bite! I guess you can see that I was not a happy camper although I lived until I was fourteen in a house without conveniences. But I guess that was different as it was our home. We had the best of two worlds. Just half a mile to the beach and a few blocks from my beloved Shrewsbury River where Papa would rent a rowboat all day for 50 cents. No wonder our house in summer was always full of N.Y. City relatives!

I understand from an article I read that Mr. Gelhaus of Keansburg had an amusement area with a carousel at his dock in the Highlands. I remember on warm evenings Mama and I would take the Patten Line from Long Branch to the Highlands. I would get refreshments and a couple of rides on the carousel and we'd take the last boat back. All this provided Mama had some extra shekels, which wasn't too often.

—Elizabeth S. Smith

HIGHLANDS FOR VACATION

The Highlands was once the favorite vacation spot for many city folks. As soon as school closed whole families, together with their trunks, descended on the boarding houses, bungalows and hotels. They came by train or steamboat.

The father of the family came along to get them settled but stayed only a couple of days before returning to work in the city. After that he rejoined his family only on weekends and for his vacation.

Many local families who had one or two bedrooms to spare took in boarders. These were usually couples who came for their two week vacation. Then they returned home and were replaced by another couple.

There were many bungalows like the row extending along one side of the Conners property. (Gravelly Point and the Conners bungalows). They were popular and were usually rented to the same families every year. Along Bay Ave. between the bridge and Shrewsbury Ave. were two rows of bungalows owned by Mr. Thomas Cashion and Mr. Chris Williams. Further up town were the ones owned by Kieferdorf and Sales. For several years there was even a tent colony along the river.

A few hotels were situated along the water front but the best known were the three large ones on Navesink Ave. (Route 36) near the bridge. They were the Highland House, the Monmouth, and the Victoria. When we walked to the beach on Saturday evenings we always walked on that side of the street so we could admire the ladies sitting on the front porch in rockers with their full skirts spread out around them. The men walked around in full dress. Chinese lanterns hung from the porch supplied the lighting.

One night the Highland House burned down. It was a most spectacular fire and most of the town gathered to watch. It was never rebuilt. The Victoria eventually became a restaurant and had many names and owners. It is now closed. The Monmouth House is now a boarding house for men and has lost its old glory. (Now the Monmouth House, too, has closed, they tell me.)

—Ann McNeill

Happy Times in the Summer

The warm days arrived early. After school on Friday five of us drove to the Jersey shore. We needed $2.50 a piece and Fred Grimsey. The money was for the gas and food. Grimsey had the Pierce Arrow.

He paid a clear $35 for it and it was a big and open and mobile as a barn in a tornado. The radiator leaked, but we carried pails of water on the floor. We also filled the radiator with oats. Blue bells grew out of that car.

Three of us were sixteen, so we knew everything. Jack Dundas was 17; he smoked. Al Porter was a brain. He had pale skin and china blue eyes so we called him Pig Puss. Bill Drummond had wavy hair; his old lady owned the bungalow.

The Necessaries

All of us packed. We took a toothbrush, a pair of shorts, sox, and from under the mattress, a copy of "La Vie Parisienne." The magazines were in case the nights were cold.

Grimsey jazzed that bird up to 30 and put his peak cap on backwards. We flew. When we reached South Amboy, we figured we were at the shore. At Water Witch we turned up Bay Avenue to Miller Street, and made a left to the Shrewsbury River.

The bungalow was 20 feet above high tide. The place looked like a retired peach crate. Nobody had to open the windows to get air. We took off our shoes and sox and rolled up our pants legs. On the out-going tide the river was black and swift and cold and ran straight up to Sandy Hook. When it saw the ocean, it did a double take and ran back.

The sand was full of busted clam shells. The skiffs riding at anchor smelled of fish and seaweed. On the opposite shore was a spit of sand. Beyond that was the Atlantic Ocean.

Two of us did the shopping for food. We bought two boxes of Cornflakes, four loaves of bread, and twenty Hershey bars. Fred Grimsey didn't have pimples. This made us think he was peculiar, except he had the Pierce Arrow, which automatically made him okay with us.

We swam and froze. Then we ate. Then we asked Grimsey to tell us again—for the 15th time—what is was like to be with a girl. We always had to coax him.

At night we slicked down our hair with Vaseline and walked up to Perry's Merry-Go-Round. Perry's was the biggie. It had penny machines with steam shovels and pinball machines and a carousel which played the "Poet and Peasant Overture" and a Strauss waltz. It didn't exactly play them—it clanked in time.

We spread out to rap the local girls, who were tired of the fishy smell of the local boys and wanted to know what life was like in the big city. They were all 14; we hunted the ones with lipstick because we knew what THAT meant.

The weekend was high adventure. If Grimsey let us use the back seat, we necked. Under the old stars, it got so hot a guy could suffocate. But we respected the girls. We called it respect; truthfully, we were scared to death.

We took them on the carousel at a nickel a rattle and we leaned way out from the horses to catch the brass ring. There was nothing we wouldn't do to impress the chicks. Everybody looked like somebody else. You could tell a girl she looked like Theda Bara—even if she looked like a can of worms. She'd call you "Sheik."

Those were dangerous words, full of innuendo. God knows where it would lead. When we ran out of nickels, we would walk across the Jersey Central bridge to Highland Beach and sit on the seawall. A fellow could always have a lot of fun helping a girl up.

Saturday was warm. And Sunday, too. At night we argued over who got the blanket. It was an army job from an old war. The bungalow had a kerosene lamp. If the wick was turned down, we went blind. If we turned

"For a day's outing go to Highland Beach. Surf and still bathing, rowing, sailing, fishing, all popular amusements, first class restaurant, merry-go-round, gravity railroad, shooting gallery, photograph gallery, lawn tennis, croquet, archery, family dressing room 50 cents, bathing suit rental 25 cents, Shrewsbury Dinners 50 cents and $1.00." *From a 1900 advertisement.*

it up, we figured the bungalow would go up with it. Molly Kirwin rented it. She let us use it on May weekends.

A Rainy Dip

We played poker for pennies. Sometimes it rained and Al Porter said the swimming was better when it rained. It wasn't. The five of us came out of the water skinny blue. We took what was left and gave it to Grimsey for the gas. That heap garbled gas faster than water. Going home we looked at our arms to see if we got tan. We threw the French magazines out as we passed the Reformatory at Rahway.

All of us are still around except Drummond. He died young. Molly kept the junky bungalow. Then she went, too. It's still there, on Miller Street. I hope some kids get some fun out of it.

—Jim Bishop

THE BEACH

Once upon a time where the old railroad bridge joined the entrance to Sandy Hook there was a narrow, sandy strip of land. It was called, affectionately by all, "the Beach." Whenever relatives came from the city to visit, the first place they wanted to go to was "the Beach." Children begged their mothers to take then there so that they could play in the nice, white sand. When teenagers gathered to decide what to do for entertainment the solution usually was "let's walk to the Beach."

On the ocean side there was a boardwalk about 200 feet in length. There were backless benches on both sides so that one could sit and watch the ocean waves or face the other way and watch the people wandering back and forth. There were several buildings owned and operated by Bill Sandlass. Between one of the bigger ones, which was a bar and grill, and the boardwalk there was a railroad track leading to Sandy Hook. Trains ran at regular intervals bringing the [civilian] workers down to Sandy Hook and back. It also transported the soldiers and their families. (At one time my

Besides movies, vaudeville-style acts and dancing, the sharp entertainer Bill Sandlass packed the "air-drome" with audiences to listen to "sacred music" played by notable bands and orchestras on Sundays, when events of other days were forbidden by the local police.

William Sandlass, founder and manager of Highlands Beach Resort, later Sandlass Beach, on Sandy Hook between the National Park entrance and the present bridge. Shown here during his visit to Cuba where he purchased and brought back native palms, bamboo lumber and fabric to create the famous Bamboo Gardens and Bamboo Room. Today, from the original dozen or so buildings, only one remains to mark the site, the Sandlass house, adjacent to the bridge and in danger of becoming derelict. *Courtesy Susan Sandlass Gardiner.*

cousin, Charles McGarry, worked as part of the crew on the train going into Sandy Hook.)

On the river side there was a row of bath houses. Using them gave you the privilege of bathing in either the river or the ocean. Near the entrance to the complex was the Bamboo Garden. It was a large one story building with a palm tree growing in the center. The space around the tree was a dance floor. Tables and chairs (made out of bamboo) were arranged around the edge of the room. There young people could stay for an entire evening, eating ice cream, drinking sodas, and dancing. It was a dress up place and we always wore our nicest clothes and were on our best behavior.

Whole families came to the beach. The parents relaxed in the sun and the children dug and played in the sand. Afterwards they all would enjoy the lunch they had brought with them or purchased on the grounds. Every summer picnic trains arrived at the Highland Beach station carrying folks from Elizabeth and Newark.

A few hundred yards up the beach toward Sea Bright was the Merry-Go-Round. It was a delightful place. The horses and other animals were so colorful and the music so pleasant. The space around the carousel was filled with rocking chairs and benches where parents could sit around and watch their children or where one could just wander in and relax for a while.

Gone! All of this wonderful playground has long since disappeared. There is no trace of any of it, except in the hearts of those who knew it and loved it.

—Ann McNeill

Family, Friends and Summertime Fun

My earliest recollection of the Highlands was about age four. I spent a week's vacation every summer with my aunt who had a house on Shrewsbury Avenue. When I was eighteen I learned my husband, John Briody's mother rented a bungalow in Quasts (now Honeysuckle Lodge) and that's where he spent his summer. After we were married we also rented there and came to Gravelly after Mom died in 1950. Mr. Giles was the owner. Our first bungalow was Herpich's (now Doyle's). Stayed there a few summers, then #47, #67 and finally bought #69. We had four castro convertables in one big room, with draw curtains on plain pipes, the ultimate.

It's difficult to recall all our good times; they were numerous. I wished my life away for the "Good Old Summer Time." Johnny and I always considered ourselves lucky to have found such wonderful friends. They remain today just as dear: Kathy, Bill, Dianne, John, Mary & Gip, Audrey & Walt, top of the list who made my loss so much more bearable by insisting and including me in everything. I will never forget them for their kindness, even our recent trip to Sailfish Point in Stewart, Florida.

We were able to walk behind my house to Mr. & Mrs. Houston on Conners. We enjoyed the Melleys in July, Kathy & Bill's family in August, Mr. & Mrs. Houston, Sr. came weekends. I loved hearing Mr. Houston's stories about the good old days and Tent City.

Our gang usually played Password one night on each weekend, then went for dancing and dinner in Conners. Who could ever forget Audrey Bluhm standing on the bar singing "God Bless America."

One night comes to mind. It was a traveling party, that is, cocktails in Dianne's, Linda Bluhm was our bunny waitress; my house for soup and salad; Audrey's for fondue; and Kathleen's for cherry cheese cake and coffee. We had a ball.

Colleen, Kim and Jeanine loved visiting Nanny and Pop Brock (as young children). She was the Nanny they never had and spoiled them with her generosity. Mrs. Mahoney sat on her porch with a supply of lollipops for all the children on the road. I remember Marty Mahoney with his bow tie and Panama hat. Quite a handsome guy. Who can forget dear Mrs. Flood and Aunt Kitty and Jack Moore, walking down the road, always had time to chat and say hello?

Bungalow Day was always the most exciting for the kids. They're all memorable especially when awarded Athlete of the Day. Can't fail to mention the Shrewsbury Beach Club Golf Classic. Gip Geffken did a super job of planning the day, charting handicaps, and cumulating prizes and trophies for the players. We anxiously awaited news of the winner. That evening we usually went to the Alpine Hotel and celebrated with the victor. One year Tommy Flynn won and Mr. Mahoney thought he cheated! In 1969, Johnny (better known as "Big Beam") was the winner. John Krahnert named Johnny Big Beam" after he installed a solid oak beam about 20' x 12" in our bungalow ceiling single-handed (except for me holding the ladder). This remained an incident he was always teased about.

Though several changes have transpired physically and aesthetically on our beach and road, it's still the place I want to be. In the confines of my little bungalow I had the most fun and happiness of my life. Sharing love and friendship with my family, grandchildren and friends, and the greatest people ever.

—Marie Briody

Kids Just Want to Have Fun

If you were a boy like Bob Herpich and spent the whole summer long in a bungalow at Gravelly Point, Water Witch, Highlands, you had lots of good times, although you didn't do anything really special or exciting, but you had fun doing it all, nonetheless.

Much of our time was spent on or in the water. Swimming was second nature to us there on a Gravelly Point. Frequently "boys only" would row to Sandy Hook, walk along the seawall to the open beach, doff our bathing suits and go swimming in the ocean.

My big thing was to swim from Spermaceti Cove to Gravelly Point at least once a summer, of course, accompanied by an adult in a rowboat. This took about twenty minutes. As for swimming, why Memorial Day was the traditional start of the swimming season, regardless of the weather. Naturally we always had to wait an hour after meals before going swimming, for that was the rule our mothers had us believe and obey.

In 1931 Bill Donovan got a South and Jersey sneakbox rigged for sailing. Bill re-rigged it and reworked the whole thing and named it the "Albatross." He and I had many happy times sailing the most infamous of which I remember well. We left Gravelly with some lunch at about nine in the morning. It was a beautiful, clear day with a good breeze. We sailed as far as Keansburg and our next tack headed us for Sandy Hook. There was some chop to the water and we did ship some water so that when we were ready for lunch we found the sandwiches were soggy with salt water. Some distance out the tiller broke. We jury rigged and decided the best place to head for was the end of the Hook. The Coast Guardsmen there helped us make a temporary repair. Well by now the sun was quite low in the sky and the wind was down to a light breeze. We started home, making a very slow headway. It got dark. The breeze died to a dead calm. Fortunately we did have oars; but a sneakbox with a centerboard is not a convenient thing to row. The tide was on the ebb and dead against us. Around midnight we finally reached Gravelly point. Both our families and lots of others where there anxiously waiting on the pier. They were just about to call the Coast Guard. I think they were so relieved to see us that we got off fairly easily.

Another time three or four of us took off in the morning with lunch and rowed up the Navesink River to Red Bank. We ate our lunch under the Cooper Bridge and then rowed back to Gravelly. Sometimes we didn't have to row at all. When the Red Bank and Long Branch steamers went along and they created quite a high stern wave some 25 feet behind the boat. If we happened to be near the channel as a steamer passed we would row in the fast and close and get on the forward side of the wave and ride it like a surfboard.

In the early 1930's there was not much military security on Fort Hancock and Sandy Hook. We went there frequently to swim, dig bait, and generally roam and explore. Once we came upon, quite unexpectedly, one of the batteries where one of the large disappearing guns was mounted. No one was around. We had a great time playing on it, turning the wheels and moving the levers.

Generally once each year the whole family would row over to Plum Island and pick the ripe beach plums that grew plentifully there. My mother would make these up into a delicious jelly that somehow never seemed to last long enough around the house.

We also did things other than in or on the water. Sometimes we would walk over to Sandlass Beach (Highland Beach) in the evening and watch the ocean. If we happen to get on the bridge, which then was a swing drawbridge, when it had to open for a boat, the bridge tender would let us ride on it as it swung open for a boat to pass.

At times during the day we would gather driftwood for an evening bonfire on the beach by the marsh. We would go to Sweeney's store and buy a few and I mean few, for they were expensive and we kids never had much money, marshmallows to roast. Often we'd get a white potato or two from the house to make "Mickeys." Now a Mickey was a white potato placed into the coals of the bonfire and roasted until the outside was charcoal black and about one eighth of an inch thick. By then the inside was steaming hot and soft. Then we ate them charcoal and all and sometimes with a little sand too.

The "Pirate Stairs" leading from the beach up to the road some sixty feet above were believed by summer children in Water Witch to have been used by pirates and smugglers in Revolutionary War days. Whatever the truth, they were great fun to climb.

Being out after dark was fun in itself. And boy was it dark since there was extremely little artificial light. The sky was black and the stars seemed close enough to touch and there were many shooting stars. And the rotating beam of the Twin Lights tower was constantly there. If mosquitoes or sand gnats were bad we would throw some eel grass into the fire to create a dense smoke that would drive them away.

We would walk the tracks to Atlantic Highlands and go to the amusement park there, which had a roller-coaster and other fun rides. We returned home late at night by bus.

The Marine Theater was open in the summers only. The building now occupied by the Lusty Lobster fish store on Bay Avenue was the movie house. I remember seeing the "Lost Battalion" there. This is the great story of an army unit in World War One surrounded by the enemy and yet saved because a carrier pigeon cut through the enemy lines with a message calling for help. The carrier pigeons were part of the Signal Corps based at Fort Monmouth where for many years they kept a pigeon that had lost one leg in a World War One battle. The pigeons were discontinued some years ago.

We used to go "exploring" through the woods up in the hills. There were the Pirate Stairs which were set of field stone steps going up from the bay to the top of the hill, with a legend that pirates used them to get to the hilltop for a lockout. Just believing that made the climb an adventure.

One day we started out on an aimless walk, that grew and grew and eventually took us to Stone Church, Locust, across the Oceanic Bridge to Rumson, then in to Sea Bright, and back to Highlands and home in Gravelly Point. That's a distance of about fifteen miles and we were a little late getting home for supper that day.

There was a little entertainment area with wheels, refreshments, etc. all clustered around the merry-go-round which was located near where the Bootlegger tavern is now. The carousel still had brass rings and we always tried to reach out and snatch one. Sometimes we caught hop toads which were quite a prolific, lightning bugs and fiddler crabs with their one big claw that could give you an uncomfortable pinch if you were not fast in grabbing them. Summers and Gravelly Point as a kid were a happy time for me.

—Robert Herpich

LIFE ON A HOUSEBOAT

Nancy May Downs, a seasonal Highlander from Jersey City, is noteworthy for her unusual boardinghouse named the Nancy-May, a houseboat popular with certain types of summer visitors who wanted to be near the water for fishing and crabbing and just plain relaxation, being rocked to sleep and far removed from the bustle and annoyances of landlubber visitors. She docked it at Highland Beach, where in September 1916, the Nancy May was voted the most popular boardinghouse at the annual Masked Ball of six hundred persons held in the Bamboo Garden on Highlands Beach. Nancy May Downs is the lady in white under the word rooms.

A number of families and married couples—we usually do not take individual men or women—spend the whole summer or just a few weeks on the Shrewsbury River. Most are regulars. We have a row boat which they use to go to and from the shore, either Highland Beach or Highlands itself. Our guests say it's one good time after another, envied by "landlubbers" who have to work and swelter on a hot humid day. Fishing right from home, crabbing, rowing and bathing just a jump into the water are the popular pastimes. Most of the boats have a Victrola for musical pleasure. Insurance agents, book salesmen and bill collectors are unknown to the people on a houseboat like the Nancy-May on the Shrewsbury.

—Nancy May Downs

The *Nancy-May* houseboat anchored near Highland Beach, with Nancy May Downs pictured in white under the word "rooms."

Come September

Come September the summer crowds emptied out by Labor Day. People who owned the bungalows and hotels and boarding houses and all the other summer businesses, they would all celebrate their going back to the cities by banging on pots and pans, and honking horns and ringing bells. They were damn glad to have them in summer for the money and all and they were even more damn glad to be rid of them in the fall.

—John A. Bahrs

On the Gravity Railroad! Just imagine the excitement and the screams of the ladies, one hand holding onto the car and one holding onto their hats, as the car plummeted at what then was breakneck speeds. How many ladies (and perhaps men, too) had to be revived from a swoon at the bottom of the ride, with men patting their cheeks, calling their names and fanning them with straw hats or handkerchiefs. Oh, the excitement!

Part 5

Hard Times

The Water Came Up Fast

John Tomasulo recounted this experience, sometimes with a slight stutter as a result of the great emotional trauma he had been through, as we sat in the dining room of his home at 49 Washington Street, Highlands. On May 17, 2001, at age forty-seven, John passed away unexpectedly, doing what he liked best, talking over Highlands history, surrounded by friends.

The water came up fast. I think no one expected it would happen like it did. This was the northeast storm that hit Highlands, December 11–12, 1992. The town did all it could to prepare people for the approaching storm. The weather reports predicted a typical nor'easter. Lots of heavy rain, high winds and coastal flooding. As the storm formed and strengthened into a monster, people all over lower Highlands began moving furniture and valuables up off the ground, off the floor, out of the reach of possible flood tides. The elementary school on the highway was getting set up as an evacuation center for people who needed a safe place to stay and had no friends or relatives to stay with 'til the storm had passed.

Highlands had been through many, many storms and floods over its history. Old timers knew what could happen. We all hoped it wouldn't. Clammers had their boats ready in case they were needed for rescue. The first aid, firemen, police and emergency management in Borough Hall

Widespread flooding, more than three feet in places, was the result of a slow-moving northeast storm on March 6, 1962. This should have been opening day of the Parrot, the popular eatery of Laura (Hartsgrove) and Vinny Renzo.

were ready for the worst. The sound trucks drove up and down all the streets downtown here blasting powerful warnings to move your cars and such up above, like around where you live and higher up even, in Henry Hudson's parking lot. People tended to leave their cars and valuables locked in them out of the possible flood but as close to home as possible. That's a natural reaction. You want things close, and you got to walk back to the house.

The storm was getting pretty worse. So I had Holly and the kids pack up some stuff, some food, you know, and blankets and pillows, and some extra clothes and move the car and get into the school as soon as possible.

I said that I would stay. Maybe it would not be so bad after all. And what could happen? I could just ride it out and go upstairs to the second floor, if the water came, as I knew it would. Look how close I am here to the boat basin. What's that? Fifty feet away? I'd be okay. It was Holly I was worried about and having the kids okay and safe. She was worried about me. What if something happened to me? My heart? What if she couldn't contact me, or what if I couldn't contact anyone outside for help?

So then the next day, I watched as the water came up and covered the street and the yard around the house. Things were floating all around all over. It was up to about the second step of the stoop. It was deep enough for a couple of boats with outboards to start moving around looking to help people. That's when I should have left, yelled to one of them and just got into the boat. Probably wouldn't even have got my sneakers wet. I guess the water was pretty cold, being December and wintertime. I think we lost power. I know now I should have cut the electricity off at the panel box. The water was seeping in under the front and back porch doors. Next it was maybe a foot deep on the floor. I had to decide then and there. I could leave while the water outside was, say, three feet deep. Would it go higher? If it did, then no way could I walk out. I put on a jacket. Got my wallet and money. The back door opened easily. Ever so carefully I held the doorjamb and stepped down into the cold water. It was about up to my waist. I knew it wouldn't be so deep if I got to Bay Avenue. I could follow the sidewalk. I'd be okay.

Then suddenly it was like I had stepped down into a hole or a ditch. The water all of a sudden was up to my armpits. I got scared. It was so cold. I think my teeth must have been chattering. I didn't know what to do. Then a boat came near and saw me, saw me in trouble. They came over. Right there on Washington Street. The guys in the boat saw that no way could they pull

Bay Avenue, true to its name, here deeply flooded its entire length with northeast storm-driven water from Sandy Hook Bay on December 11–12, 1992. *Courtesy Historical Society of Highlands and Shoregrafx.*

me, my size, into that boat. They had me hold on to the side, my elbows in the boat, and they guided me into lower and lower water. I must have been almost over by the bank before I was in water only to my knees or ankles. Some first aid people, I think from another town, maybe, got me into a truck and up to Henry Hudson—cause the grade school roof got damaged—and dry and warm and safe.

See that line around the wall? Well, it's hard to see it now. The repairmen did such a neat job. Perfect. You'd never know the water in this room was close to three feet over the floor. All over Bay Avenue the water was three and almost four feet deep. It crashed in the plate glass windows in the Sand Dollar. The sirens I heard were for the three houses at the end of Gravelly Point. The firemen could do nothing but watch from far away. The engines could not go through water that deep. The houses raised off the foundations, and the gas lines broke. Something sparked, and they just burned almost down to the water before the gas company could turn the lines off there and all over down town here, too late.

We're all okay now. Thanks to the insurance. Thanks to God.

—John Tomasulo, from an interview with John P. King, Spring 1995

BAD TIMES

Gina Smith is a twenty-eight-year-old mother of three children, speaking about her life in Highlands. All names have been changed.

This place is a wreck. I need a new rug, and I need a new floor. I have to use a bucket every time I do a load of wash. The machine don't work. I had a fire in my wall the other day. Somethin' happened in the wall. The refrigerator plug got on fire. It blew the electric out upstairs, and it don't work. It burned it all out. This whole side of the kitchen.

I don't get child support. I get welfare. I get $488 a month and $200 in food stamps. The rent is $400, my electric is $30 and gas $50 a month. If I go by the book, I don't have any cigarette money and I don't have money for soap, bleach, nothin'. It's like I have to rent the extra room to survive. I tried to rent the room for $75 a week, and I do the wash. I had my brother, George, live here. Robbie Jones lived with me for a while. He did all the paintin' here, as a matter of fact. Don Viola used to live with me. He was rentin' a room off me. Four years. I rented a room to everybody in this town.

I was goin' to rent the room to Larry, then we started goin' together, and he gives me his paycheck, and that's even better.

Larry ain't sick in the head. He ain't crazy. He gives me his paycheck to pay the bills. He gives me money. He don't smack me around. We can drink together and not kill each other. My kids love 'im, and he holds 'em, and he talks to 'em.

I'm $1,800 in debt. Well, I had to pay rent, and I didn't have any money for school. I took my check and went out and bought school clothes. That's $400. Bad debt. Birthdays and stuff like that, you know. Bad debts. Larry just called the landlord and told 'im he'd have a thousand dollars for 'im on the first. So, he's payin' it off. You know, if I need sneakers or somethin' for the kids, I can just go out and buy them now. If he moved out, I'd have to rent the room to somebody else.

Welfare. They'd cut my check right off, if they knew about me rentin' the room. You ain't allowed to have nobody livin' with you. You ain't allowed to have a bank account or a car. If you do, they decrease your check.

To save money, I get most of my clothes from the Salvation Army bags. We go over to the Salvation Army bins at K-mart and take the bags out and bring 'em home. That's where I get all my shoes for the kids and all and all Stacy's school clothes come outa there. I get coats and shit outa there, man. I got some nice ski jackets. One time I found $20 in a coat pocket.

I go to the garbage can to get a lot of stuff. Go garbage pickin.' I got that bar out of the garbage. Rumson garbage is good. They throw everythin' out. You get all kinds of good shit. All kinds of stuff I find in it. I think the only thing in this house I paid for is that microwave over there. Everythin' else I got out of the garbage or my grandmother gave me. The TV I got because Tom Davidson was livin' here, and he didn't pay his rent so I got his TV.

We used to come down here in summers. Then we moved here when I was nine years old. We had the movie house and everythin'. Then we used to have a good time. We used to come down here and bowl at the Red Rooster. I remember goin' to the beach, barbecuin', eatin' lobster on the weekend. All of us hangin' out by the beach, havin' good times. I had some wild good times too. Everybody hangin' out, goin' to the ocean, all of us cruisin' around together. Cruisin' around Friday nights. It was great. Parties, wetdowns. I love 'em. It's not like it used to be though.

Life is tough. Too much aggravation and too many bills I can't pay. Take me away, get me outa here. I can't give my kids what they want and need. I get tired of it. Christmas I didn't have a damn thing in this house, nothing' for my kids. I did get one thing a piece for my kids. We didn't even have a

Christmas tree. The VFW come over with a tree and the American Legion brought me lights and all. Churches come down with presents. Toys for the kids. They brought food. I was embarrassed. They knocked on the door, and Frank Michelson's father came and hollered, "Santa Claus is here." The room was filled with toys. I had four Santa Clauses that day. I guess people gave 'em my name. I said, "Holy shit! How embarrassin." And they had a good Christmas after all and I said, "Oh, my God!" You feel like so embarrassed because I couldn't do it myself, and it was nice to know that somebody else gives a shit.

I'd like to get off of welfare. Maybe if I get lucky enough to get married one of these days and get someone to take care of me. I ain't smart enough to work. The only job I ever had was babysittin.' I worked in a McDonald's, but you only get $3 an hour. I never worked a cash register in my life. I don't know how to fill out a job application. They think you're an idiot in there. You're twenty-eight years old, and you don't know how to work a cash register.

This Christmas? Who knows. I have no idea. I don't even know for sure if we'll even have food. I know Larry will get them school clothes. I have to worry about three of them this year. Donnie goes to school this year. Stacy's class went on a trip to Great Adventure, and I didn't have the money to send my kid, and she really wanted to go. She cried all day. Things like that really hurt me, things they really want. I remember when I was a kid wantin' to go somewhere. My mother didn't have the money to send in to school. I cried. Then I had to hear the other kids say, "Yeah, we went to Philadelphia yesterday, and it was great!" Now Christmas is too far away to worry about it.

There's some good things about life in Highlands. But you can't really have fun in this town. Everybody's so two-faced and backwards. It's nice that you can go to the beach every day because it's in walkin' distance. I also liked the fact that I know everybody. I like that I can walk down the street at eleven o'clock at night and not have to worry about gettin' mugged. It's clean too, not like you're walkin' in the city and seein' shit all over the place. I'd like to keep it clean—no niggers, you know, I'm prejudiced.

Maybe since I was a kid, I haven't had a favorite moment. I haven't had a good moment in a long time, a real long time, not in so long. Shit!

—Gina Smith, from an interview by Richard Maxson Jr.

World War II and Highlands: "Dear Pop"

Corporal Robert Maynard Cottrell, paratrooper, was wounded June 8 in the invasion of France. He wrote the following letter from a hospital in England to his father, William R. Cottrell, of Fourth Street, telling of being wounded, taken prisoner by the enemy and how, a few days later, the Ninth Division boys captured the German hospital where he was located at the time.

August 15, 1944.

Dear Pop,

Just a note to let you know everything is under control. My wound has healed up very nicely, although I am back in bed with a little temperature, I really feel O.K. I should be up in a few more days. Those damned Nazi bastards shot me in the lower part of the chest. The bullet went clean through, so I consider myself lucky. I had quite a time over there. It reminded me of a good day's duck shoot. I know I got more than my share of them. After they shot me (we were ten miles behind their lines), they made me walk about a mile-and-a-half to their headquarters, where they took everything off me, including my first aid packs, then they tore up all my invasion money. They put me with some other of our boys and we slept in a ditch for a day and one-half before they took us to a so called hospital. There they had some more of our men, and a few of our First Aid men who fixed up our wounds. They didn't treat us too badly; I guess they didn't have much to offer. They gave us some kind of soup once a day and some terrible bread and cheese. There was bombing and shelling from our own troops just a few yards from the hospital, so we knew the Germans would soon get the hell out of there. They didn't move fast enough, because on the sixth day the Ninth Division boys came and captured the hospital. I was sent to two different field hospitals in France and finally sent to England by plane. I received letters from Pauline, Naomi and Evelyn since I've been the hospital, but no mail that was sent to my company. There isn't anything I need, even though haven't been paid for three months. I didn't feel like smoking until a week ago, and I can get cigarettes from the Red Cross. Well, Pop, after I take one more crack at those yellow dogs, just to even up the score, maybe I'll be seeing you soon. Take things easy now. Lots of love to you and the family.

Your son, Maynard.

Part 6

Prohibition Days

Confession of a Rumrunner

I can't say I'm proud of what I did, but hard economic times left me little choice or me and my family could have lost the business and everything else too. I was only 16 years old when I started in this business in 1928. I operated out of St. Pierre and Miquelon, islands actually part of France, but overseas, off the coast of Newfoundland. Seldom did I work Rum Row off the coast here in the Highlands. When prices were low, as they occasionally were in the late 1920s, we could buy top quality Scotch whiskey there for as little as $6 or $7 a case with a great resale value back home. Up there we also could buy pure grain alcohol 180 proof at $4 for six gallons. It would have flavors added and sold to speakeasies and private people as gin. Other flavors and coloring would transform the stuff into "whiskey."

Some liquor came from the West Indies, mainly rum and principally from Cuba. I made only one trip down there. We went down with a bunch of wooden kegs that had been disassembled and when we got to Cuba they were put back together again and filled with rum. We paid $1.50 for each six gallons of rum. By the time I was 22 in 1934, I had made nine rumrunning trips on schooners carrying 2,500 to 3,000 cases from Canada, two to Highlands off Sandy Hook and the rest to places in Maine. During Prohibition's last years diesel powered coastal freighters carried as many as 5,000 cases. This business was largely controlled by the big city mobsters.

When Prohibition started anybody with even a row boat could get in on the game if he had the cash to buy. Sometimes on calm nights we landed loads of stuff right through the surf in rowboats at Sea Bright. I could go out and buy about 10 cases for the rowboat.

At first in the earliest days guys would work Rum Row as independent operators but soon they got together and formed small combinations of five or six boats that they worked as an "outfit." When the returning boats rounded the Hook, other boats that had been hiding out in the darkness and without any liquor would speed out as decoys for the Coast Guard patrol boats and trick them to follow as far as Staten Island. Meanwhile, the boats with liquor headed to their landing places and unloaded their cases.

The boats used were maybe fifty feet long and powered with two powerful gasoline engines to give them high speed with heavy loads. They were painted gray and since they ran only on moonless nights and without running lights, they were practically invisible on the water.

Near the end of Prohibition we used other tricks. We had a little pilot house up near the bow of the boat, fastened down with turn buckles. We would take that off and move it to the stern, then, if search lights reflected

Rumrunners, names unknown or not mentioned, here in taunting operation just out of reach of the Coast Guard. The location of Highlands near New York City and the shipping lanes, combined with experienced local watermen, made the town the ideal port of the illegal trade.

off the glass of the pilot house, the Coast Guard gunners would aim at that and we wouldn't be hit.

Then there was old Cap ——, I won't say his name. He owned a popular establishment here in Highlands before he died. Back then he was the Captain of the Coast Guard over there at Sandy Hook. He got a quarter of a case for every case that come in around the Hook. It was all arranged. He'd be given word that the boats were coming in so he'd send the Coast Guardsmen to Coney Island or Rockaway. So the guys would come in home free. It was amazing. Of course, nobody ever hurt anybody. Well, a couple of guys got killed, unfortunately, but when you figure the percentages, it seemed to work out all right.

—Anonymous
mid-1990s

Bootleggers

Prohibition made so many changes in our peaceful little town. It became a Mecca for rum runners who came to take advantage of the many hidden coves where boats could be unloaded unseen. As for the natives, greed and excitement overcame the law abiding nature of many as they joined the ranks of the outlaws.

High powered boats put out to sea in the darkness to meet up with large boats waiting off shore. They transferred the cargo and raced for shore hoping to out run the Coast Guard. However, they also had fast boats and guns too. Often I woke in the night to the sound of gunfire and wondered what neighbor's son would not be coming home next day. One such case was a young man named Kadenback. He left a wife and child.

At all hours of the day and night speedy cars headed for Canada, some driven by women. They returned by way of the back roads with their loads, hoping to avoid the law.

The Coast Guard was not the only one with guns. Armed hijackers toured the highway and sometimes a cargo from Highlands changed hands more than once. Sometimes there was blood shed.

A young couple from Newark, the Bill Smiths, rented the garage apartment across from our back gate (on Valley Ave.). His older brother, Neil, rented a house farther up Valley Ave. They were both active bootleggers and had many young men helpers, well dressed and polite.

One day word was passed around that there was going to be a raid. Two of the well-mannered young men arrived at our back door and asked if we could use some wood. With three wood-burning stoves, of course we could. They went away and returned with a load of wooden liquor boxes which they proceeded to break up and stack up in our barn. Evidence disposed of, we had fire wood for a long time.

During this time I was teaching in Atlantic Highlands. One of my fifteen year-old girls was offered $10 an hour to tutor a young boy in math. The family lived high up in the hills. Each day during the summer a car arrived to take the girl to her pupil. It wasn't until later that she learned that it was bullet-proof. As she arrived one day she happened to glance at the house; there up on the cat-walk was a young man parading with a gun. After the lesson that day she explained that she had to go away and couldn't continue the lessons. However, she did mourn the loss of the $10.

—Ann McNeill, 1989

DANGEROUS BUSINESS

During Prohibition times, one particular night I went out to Rum Row, where all the boats loaded with whiskey and such laid off shore outside of Coast Guard jurisdiction. But I couldn't find the schooner I was after, but I found another one and on this schooner was a guy there, wanted to come back to shore. So this Dutch Whitey come on board my boat and he had a suitcase. In this suitcase was $250,000. We landed this guy at Bahrs landing. Christmas eve and he gave us a case of Canadian Club apiece for bringing him ashore and he kept the $250,000. There was big money being made in rumrunning those days.

I can remember one other time I went off shore to get a load of liquor and I got off three nights straight in a row. This night, this fellow sent his brother with me to tell us where to land. So in place of landing where we been landing which is the old Patten Line dock we landed near Conners Hotel. So here comes the Coast Guard walking down the dock and we got a couple hundred cases of liquor. So I pull away and laid in the channel cause I knew they wasn't going to swim after me at this time of year. Now along comes another boat operated by Howie Lindauer. He comes along past the Patten dock and he got shot and his boat went up into the creek near the Jackson Hotel, just south of it. He got shot and his liquor was there and the

Coast Guards grabbed it but before the night was over this boat went on fire and all the liquor was burnt up and lost. This guy, Bill Price, he never paid all of the amount per case that you were supposed to get, so that's why they were laying for him and a short time after this, he was found in a sack in Brooklyn, with concrete. He was shot and killed and dumped in a bag with concrete and put a little out in the bay.

—Bill Hodge

Highlands a Hub in the Rumrunning Era

This account of the days rumrunners evaded authorities in and around Highlands to satisfy their customers' desires and to better their own financial gain all in the face of the Prohibition Laws is based on oral reports and on the personal reminiscences shared by several people and by John "Buddy" Bahrs, former mayor, restaurateur, Highlands native, but not "rumrunner."

Bahrs was just a twelve-year-old boy when Prohibition became the law nationwide on January 20, 1920. His father had been taking the family from their home in Newark to Highlands to spend the summer since 1912, and one summer, he found what he considered a great opportunity, buying a boathouse and boat rental business located on the river at the foot of Cedar Street, where the James T. White clam depurification plant stands today. Later, his father, John H. Bahrs, and mother, Florence, bought McGuire's boathouse on the site of today's Bahrs Landing Restaurant, where the whole family moved in. They actually lived, a tough life for the mother and kids, year-round in the two-story boathouse that had a half-dozen bunks on one floor and some fifty on the other, all with mattresses stuffed with cornstalks and straw. Soon weekend fishermen made Bahrs their headquarters, and the kids, Ruth, Al, Ken and Buddy, sleeping on the hard and cold bunks made it their home, without ever a complaint.

Fishermen used to pay $3.50 each for boat, bait, bunk and board provided by Florence Bahrs' good home cooking, which was served on tables covered with sheet metal. There were no menus, no tablecloths or napkins and no complaints, just thanks from the fishermen going for flounder, fluke, porgies and striped bass in the river.

The rumrunners or bootleggers made Highlands their base of illegal operations since it was the nearest New Jersey town to the offshore supply ships and since there were plenty of large, powerful and fast-moving lobster boats (refitted with very powerful war surplus airplane engines) there for easy hire to bring the whiskey contraband around the Hook and into waiting cars and trucks, having out-run any pursuing Coast Guard patrol boats. They chose Bahrs because it was right on the water, close to the ocean and offered warm hospitality, decent accommodations and good food, especially Florence's clam chowder.

While the buyers were all men from the cities with associations to a tougher criminal element in organized crime, the men who ran the boats were all locals, good seamen, hard-working lobstermen and clammers who saw nothing wrong with their participation in this victimless crime, who struggled to make ends meet even before the Depression hit and who were legitimized in their unlawfulness by the senselessness of the law that no one ever wanted, that no one respected. These Highlands men could ride out past the three-mile limit of U.S. jurisdiction, day or night, in storm or calm, to "rum row" off Highlands, Sea Bright, Monmouth Beach and Long Branch, where a small fleet of ships from Canada awaited boats carrying buyers.

While at first rumrunning boats operated boldly in broad daylight since initially there was no patrol set up to stop them, soon they had to work under cover of darkness to disguise their crime a bit. The city men would sit around one or more iron stoves in Bahrs, talking, playing cards, even reading and always waiting to find out when and where the boats were coming in with their purchases. A lookout on the rocks over at Highland Beach used binoculars and a powerful flashlight to detect and respond to prearranged signals from the boats at "rum row." Then shining his beams into Bahrs, he let the men know where to meet the boats, at Highlands, in Leonardo, in Belford or someplace else. All the men jumped up, downed their drinks or coffees and ran to their cars and trucks. They used big and fast Diamond Reo Speed Wagons, but many preferred long sedans fitted up with extra heavy-duty springs since these had the needed space, the speed and the element of disguise. With fifteen or more cases of Canadian whiskey in the backs of the cars, they could ride to the city looking just like plain, ordinary people returning from the shore.

The bootleggers who worked through Bahrs—Whitey, Dutch, Providence and Dingbat, to name some of the aliases used—respected the family and its business, were polite (especially to Mrs. Bahrs), treated the kids well and always paid their bills with generosity. However, the respect was not necessarily reciprocated. John Bahrs knew full well that what he was doing was wrong, but it was business and times were tough. He was just starting out, and he had to make a living; he had a family to feed. Many a local and many a bootlegger thought Bahrs should use his large sea skiff for a more lucrative business than the pound-net fishing it had been built for by Seaman Boats in Long Branch. They urged Jack Bahrs to get with it, to wise up, and to take the boat out and load it up with whiskey, to make a real dollar or two. He hated what he was already doing. His good wife, Florence, worried about the whole affair. She wanted no part of it, and he refused.

It seemed that everyone was into the bootlegging thing, including the officer in charge at the Coast Guard base on Sandy Hook who would get a telephone call that rum boats were coming in to Highlands. He would send his patrol and gunboats to look in a different location, say, by Perth Amboy. The men would find nothing, but he would find a quarter case of good Canadian waiting on the dock. Just about everyone in Highlands reaped the benefits of Prohibition and rumrunning. They made plenty of fast money and spent it swiftly. The women who worked in the clam shucking and stringing sheds along the river suddenly had fur coats to keep them warm in the bitterly cold huts and homes. Some even glamorously displayed new diamond rings on their fingers, like the movie starlets they saw, though their fingers were like stubs from opening clams.

From time to time, there would be raid on Highlands speakeasies. Police would swoop into several places simultaneously, and the results would be read in the papers the next Thursday—not in the *Star* or the *Journal*, the local town papers, but in the *Red Bank Register*, for example, of June 11, 1930. "County detectives made five raids at the Highlands. The owners of the places were arraigned in Freehold and held in $1,000 bail for the Grand Jury on charges of illegal possession and sale. Arrested were Tom C——, Emil A——, S. W——, Michael M——, and Frank M——." Apparently it was without public shame or disapproval that they remained in town, using their profits to finance memorial windows in the new church being built and opening legal taverns after Prohibition was over.

The glamour evaporated, the money devalued and the thrills vanished whenever a bootlegging affair went contrary to expectations. Coast Guard machine-gun bullets ripped open a man's spine in a boat headed for shore, where he died sprawled on the floor of the sedan intended for whiskey, and a man was blinded for life in an explosion, pouring naphtha instead of gasoline into a hot boat engine to make it run faster when being pursued.

With the Twenty-first Amendment to the Constitution, national Prohibition came to an end on December 5, 1933. The lobstermen returned to their lobster pots, the clammers to their boats, bushels and rakes and people to the twenty-six taverns licensed in the little borough just .64 square mile.

—John A. Bahrs, as edited by John P. King

Highlands a Center for Bootlegging

The passage of a half century has not dimmed my memories of the exciting years of Prohibition although I was only 12 when Prohibition became the law of the land on January 20th, 1920. I have almost total recall concerning the days when the Highlands was at a mecca for bootleggers and rumrunning and rumrunners. In 1912 my family began coming down from Newark to spend summers here. A few years later, my father, John H. Bahrs, bought a boat house and rowboat rental business and set up at the foot of Cedar Street. My family moved to the site of the present restaurant in 1917. What now is Bahrs restaurant was originally a double decked houseboat with several wooden bunks on the first floor and a couple of dozen on the upper floor. I remember that the mattresses were stuffed with a corn stalks and a straw. When weekend fishermen began making it their headquarters, they and, like me and my sister Ruth and my brothers Ken and Al we all slept on the hard bunks without complaint. Visiting fishermen paid my father $2.50 for the weekend, meals included, and another dollar a day to rent and their boats. Some would stay a week, fishing for striped bass, flounder, and porgies then plentiful in the river. And just like my family, they ate at a plain wooden table covered with galvanized iron because, we didn't bother much with tablecloths and napkins in those rough days.

Many of the bootleggers chose Highlands as a base because the little fishing village had plenty of fast lobster scamps suitable for burning illegal liquor in around. In the early '20s running boats operated in broad daylight, their contraband cargo covered with a piece of canvas. The local men who ran these gifts were good seamen they could ride out night or day and pick up booms from ships on Rum Row off Sandy Hook, Sea Bright, Monmouth Beach. Rum Row was a fleet of ships that brought large supplies of liquor down from Canada and anchored just outside of the 3 mi. limit of U.S. jurisdiction.

Since my father operated one of the few places with any kind of accommodations, the bootleggers stayed with us. This was more or less of their headquarters for the first couple of years of prohibition. At night the men sat around the old pot belly stove waiting to find out when and where the boats were coming in from Rum Row. The bootleggers that stayed with us carried flashlights about 2 feet long, powerful, with Red, Green and White lenses in them; one man would go across the bridge to the rocks where the Sandlass Beach Club was, just south of what's now the entrance to Sandy Hook. He signaled to the people on the ships and found out whether the booze was coming in here or up at the Belford or just where. As soon as he got to the word, all the guys would jump into their cars or trucks with their boots on because they didn't know where they were going to unload the stuff by standing in water or mud or what. Some of bootleggers drove Diamond Rio speed wagon trucks and others used sedans cars fitted with heavy-duty helper springs. They could load as many as 15 cases into the backs of those cars and ride to the city looking like plain ordinary cars going home.

Even though the bootleggers were criminals under the almost universally unpopular Volstead Act, they used often speak with a certain amount of affection, then known only by nicknames like Dutch, Whitey and Dingbat. They sometimes brought food down from the city but most of the time they ate what ever fare we had and slept in our bunk rooms. Mother did the cooking and all of us kids did chores to help out. Many of the bootleggers who were armed; some guys were what I call pretty tough characters. The only ones that got hurt, though, were the tough ones. The good guys would take care of the bad guy soon be on their way out of town. When the bootleggers stayed at my father's place they ate almost like a part of the family. They would never take anything from mother or dad, and they thought my folks were the greatest people in the world. As far as my mother and father were concerned, the feeling was not entirely mutual. My mother and father hated any part of the bootlegging business, of course, but they had to make a living. Even though Dad had his own boat, he still wouldn't use it for running liquor. In the mid 20s my father bought a pound boat to take out fishing parties. This was a large sea skiff designed to bring in fresh fish from offshore pound nets and was built by the Seaman Boats in Long Branch. I remember that several bootleggers kept telling my dad, "Come on, Jack, take that boat out and load it up with whiskey." Dad refused.

Because everything had been fixed in advance, rumrunners and bootleggers operated quite openly for some years. The federally imposed ban on alcoholic beverages provided many attractive financial opportunities for fishing communities like Highlands. When word of an incoming load was passed, a bootlegger would often inform the commander of the Coast Guard base at Sandy hook. The officer then dispatched his patrol boats to go to out of the way places like Coney Island, so they could not bother the rumrunners coming in.

I recall that just about everybody in town benefited in some way from Highlands era of prominence as a major rendez-vous point for bootleggers and rumrunners. The bootleggers and the people here who were associated with them made plenty of money and many of them spent it like water. The girls who worked in the clam shanties, for example, had fur coats and wore diamond rings on hands that looked like clubs from opening clams. Local garages and boatyards did a lively business and even the clergy got its piece of the liquor action.

—John A. Bahrs

Part 7

Highlanders, Some Famous

Jennie Parker

I knew Jennie Parker. Everyone used to call her Aunt Jennie, for people had great affection for her dedication to the sick and especially to women having babies. She lived right in the heart of old Parkertown, at Fourth and Valley. She was like a midwife, assisting Dr. Roland or Dr. Opfermann with deliveries at home. For a week before birth, she would visit the mother each day, preparing her breakfast and teaching her prenatal health care. After the birth, she would visit daily, making breakfast for the mother, sometimes preparing and leaving lunch as well, would help her [the mother] wash herself and the baby and would give basic baby care lessons as needed. Her bill for some three weeks service would typically run no more than $20, or less than $1.00 per day. Aunt Jennie helped me with two of my children. She's dead now, of course. I think she died during the war and then, of course, the housing projects were named after her.

—Estelle White
From an interview in November 1995 by Helen King

HIGHLANDS ADORED HER

Then there was Gertrude Ederle, the first woman to swim the English Channel. She learned to swim off Kruse's grove near the hotel. Her parents rented a summer cottage there. Once five children tumbled out of a row boat, and she jumped in and saved them all. When she crossed the river 22 times she figured she could tackle the Channel.

That day of the big swim the residents of Highlands lived by their radios awaiting bulletins from overseas. On her return in a huge parade she rode down Bay Ave. in a big red roadster with white wheels which was every child's impossible dream for months. We had the welcome-home dinner for her in the McGuire House and a grand ball at Kruse's pavilion. I don't think the borough has ever experienced more excitement. Even the cannons boomed on Sandy Hook. And Trudy says her heart's in the Highlands until this day.

Would I ever want to live anywhere else? Not a chance. They claim once you've seen the Highlands water and the Highlands mountain you have to come back. As for me, I have a compulsion to remain here.

—Edna Kruse

The Marine Theatre opened in 1922 and showed films only in summer. It was here that Gertrude Ederle's *Swim Girl, Swim* filled every seat in the house for showing after showing in 1926. Doug Douty's popular Lusty Lobster seafood outlet is an example of adaptive reuse and preservation.

Miss Ederle played a supporting role with the glamorous starlet Bebe Daniels in the 1926 Paramount film *Swim Girl, Swim*, something that she said annoyed her a little since she was America's star athlete, although her name and her photo in a swimsuit were always in advertisements.

MY HEART IS IN THE HIGHLANDS

"Trudy" was written by Charles Tobias and Al Sherman and published by Irving Berlin, Inc., 1926. From a single-sided record in the editor's collection.

You know, many people who have read it in print in the many, many magazine and newspaper articles written about me since my channel swim in 1926, they just can't believe it, but it is really a true story. I think I remember it most of all my time in the water. I truly did learn to swim in the Shrewsbury River, right there in Highlands. My family had a bungalow right on the water near the Patten dock by Creighton's or Kruse's. One day, my father took me and a big long rope out to the end of the dock there, tied the rope tightly around me under my arms and threw me into the river. "Swim, Trudy, swim! Swim, girl, swim!" is what he kept shouting. And so I swam, and I just kept on swimming, in Highlands and in the city. It was in Highlands, in the terribly strong and unpredictable Shrewsbury River currents just around the bridge, that I put in a lot of my training to get ready for my big swim from France across to England on August 6, 1926. My father was with me there too, and he kept shouting, "Swim, Trudy, swim!" They played music to keep my spirits up, on a crank-up gramophone. "Let Me Call You Sweetheart" was my favorite. I'll sing you some. "Let me call you sweetheart, I'm in love with you. Let me hear you whisper that you love me too....." Did you know that after I returned to America they had a ticker tape parade down Broadway for me? And Irving Berlin, the famous Irving Berlin, wrote me a song? It's called "Trudy." I'll sing it for you too.

In my neighborhood a girl named Trudy
Has the fellows running after her,
And they all feel it their duty
To call at her home and sing to this beauty.

Trudy, we always want you near us,
Trudy, when you're around you cheer us.
You've got a smile worth a million to see,
You're such a cutie, you're as sweet as Tutti Fruiti, Trudy.

Who'll be the lucky fellow?
Tell, oh tell us, please do,
Trudy, we mean it truly, ooly,
Ooly, ooly, Trudy, we love you.

Ev'ry now and then the boys would find her,
Swimming with her girl friends all around,
They'd follow closely behind her,
And when they were near,
They'd shout and remind her.

Trudy, we love our swimming daughter,
Trudy, you're like a fish in water,
You swam the channel that treacherous sea,
But you went through it,
We knew it, we knew that you could do it, Trudy.
To think a girl like you, dear,
Broke the world's record too,
Trudy, now that you've done your duty
Trudy, Uncle Sam is proud of you.

The drive from New York down to Highlands was slowed by crowds of fans all along the route wanting to see and cheer Ederle, who always said her most thrilling parade was along Bay Avenue, where her swimming career began. Note the huge American flag, for her swim and parades were patriotic events.

Gertrude Ederle, "Queen of the Waves" and "America's Best Girl," standing in celebration in her red roadster on Broadway in 1926, the adulation of all New York and the world.

I've had a good life and done many exciting things. Did you know I starred in a Hollywood movie? It was called "Swim, Girl, Swim!" Just like my father first said. And I danced with Johnny Weismeuller. Tarzan! The big New York parade was thrilling for a young girl like me. But the parade the people in the Highlands gave me was more wonderful and especially moving as we passed on Bay Ave. the place where it all began. I love the Highlands. You know, my heart is in the Highlands.

—Gertrude "Trudy" Ederle, age ninety-four in September 2000, when she was visited by the editor on two occasions. "Trudy" was written by Charles Tobias and Al Shermanand published by Irving Berlin, Inc., 1926.

GERTRUDE EDERLE

Back in the 1920's the Ederle family from New York City summered each year at the Highlands. One of their daughters, Gertrude, learned to swim in

Above: Gertrude Ederle in 1956 at Bahrs for the thirtieth anniversary of her channel swim, with an Ederle doll, Julie Donaghue Stutzman and officer Harry Duncan.

Left: Miss Ederle is shown here aboard the ship bringing her happily home after her triumphant swim and quick visit with family in Germany. She sailed with her father and sister Helen and a whole horde of newsmen and photographers. She wrote a column each day, sent by radiogram, to the *New York Daily News*.

the Shrewsbury River there. She soon became an expert. She was ambitious and thought she could do some long distance swimming. As a result on August 6, 1926 Gertrude Ederle, a 19 year-old New York native exited the water at Dover, England. She had just set a record for swimming across the English Channel. She was the first woman to do this.

The Highlands claimed her as their own. The town was decorated from one end to the other. The parade at her homecoming circled the entire town. It was led by friend Jimmy Collins in his full-dress West Point uniform.

My cousin, Margaret McDonough, from Rhode Island, was visiting me that summer and so was able to enjoy the festivities.

—Ann McNeill

John Azzolina

The Food Circus clown, a Middletown landmark since Joe Azzolina and family opened their supermarket on Route 35, shortly after the closing of the first supermarket, Food Basket, on Bay Avenue.

John Azzolina would trust the clammers all winter long. I lived in 80 Miller Street and he had the store right next door. I don't know how the house numbers were. We had an alley between us. He would trust you, and he gave us credit. When we first asked for it, he would only allow us $2 and then when he seen that we paid up the $2, then gradually he extended. And he did that for all of the clammers. At one time when John Azzolina opened the Food Basket, we had a long talk. He told me that in all of the years and years that he trusted the clammers he got stuck for less than $200.

When he opened the Food Basket, he offered anyone in the Highlands a job with him, and those that did, they stayed with him until he retired. He was an Italian man, who came from Italy. He spoke broken English, but he had a heart of gold. He was a loyal

American citizen and a loyal Highlands resident. And he always used to make his own of sausage. I can see him there doing it and I used to laugh at him because there he was standing with these long skins, you know, and stuffing in the sausage.

—Lillian Maxson, from an interview by David Maxson, 1996

Jimmy White

Jimmy White, our ex-mayor, Jimmy White helped the town an awful lot. He was a schoolteacher here in town. He was a self-educated man. When he retired from school, after earning an M.A., he became interested in the clam business again. It's family heritage, as far as I am concerned. And during the time Jimmy White was involved in the clam business, he never turned

Jimmy White, Highlands born and raised, demonstrates the use of a hoe in harvesting soft clams. He was a Highlands teacher, councilman, mayor from 1968 to 1974 and again in 1989, clammer and baymen's advocate, who died delivering clams and doing what he loved. In 1995, the clam depuration facility was named after him.

anybody down, and he was helpful to everybody, and I know that personally. He was a soft-spoken, mild-mannered gentleman, and from the time he was a little kid he was like that. He educated himself, and he graduated from Monmouth College. His main subject in the college? He graduated with a physics degree. Why he ever chose to teach in an elementary school, I could never understand why. The only reason I could ever come up with, when I used to think about it, was that he didn't want to go any further. Because he wanted to stay right in Highlands.

A small-town atmosphere, the family atmosphere is a wonderful thing, I really believe. When I first came to Highlands and times were hard, nobody ever went hungry. If a person, say for instance, my husband made more money than the next door clammer, we would always be willing to share what we had with that poor guy who was down in the dumps and had maybe about six children to feed. And that's true.

—Lillian Maxson, from an interview by David Maxson

THE HARTSHORNES

For many years before his death in 1899 grandpa [James McGarry] was superintendent of the Hartshorne estate [having followed "Squire" John Van Kirk]. Sometimes when he would come home for lunch, he would take mother and Auntie back with him to play with the two Hartshorne girls, Julia and Mary.

There was a housekeeper called Margaret that the girls were very fond of. She always had crackers and milk for them. The friendship lasted through the years and mother and Auntie were encouraged to share anything that grew in the fields or woods.

I guessed that privilege extended to me, for often Nixie, my dog, and I went over the hill to pick raspberries that grew on the edge of the farm land. Some of the finest wildflowers grew in those woods, much to my delight. Once when I was walking along a narrow path in the woods, a red fox bounded out from one side and into the brush on the other. I had been told that forest fires in south Jersey had driven many wild animals up this way. However, that was the only red fox I ever saw.

The Hartshorne girls grew up and married. Julia married Dr. Trask. They had three sons and lived in a house (a wedding gift) high on the bluff where the river bends its way to Red Bank [now Sea Scape Manor B&B]. This property was turned over to the government during World War Two and the Trasks remained in New York. Mary married an officer in the Navy by the name of Ward. One day Mary stopped to see Auntie. She had a baby in her arms. "Maggie," she said, "I want you to meet my grandson." Auntie replied, "He's lovely and the fifth generation of Hartshornes that I have seen." Later one day in a tailor shop a man introduced himself to me. He was Daniel Seitz, the baby that his grandmother had brought to see Auntie. Dan and I became good friends. I have been able to tell him things about his family that my folks told me. I've also given him clippings that they saved. I found his grandmother's wedding announcement that she had sent to mother and dad. It had been printed at Tiffany's and was in excellent condition. He was pleased to get it.

—Ann McNeill

Buddy Bahrs

"When you think of Highlands, you just have to think of Bud Bahrs," said Muriel Smith. Always full of tales about the town and the people he loved, with a twinkle in his eyes reflecting the pleasure and enthusiasm he had for Highlands, Bahrs was raised by his parents to believe that all debts were to be repaid and favors were to be balanced with gratitude.

Mayor Bahrs had no enemies, only friends with whom he occasionally disagreed, especially in politics. He respected disagreement as acceptable only if all parties were working and volunteering for the same goal, the common good of the town and people of Highlands. Bahrs maintained strict priorities throughout his life: first came family, then business and the affairs of town tied for second place. "You have to give back. You have to repay some of the good that's been done for you," Bahrs often said.

He always was of a positive and upbeat attitude, ready with praise, seldom with criticism, despite having been seriously assaulted and robbed twice in his home by armed thieves and once attacked by life threatening cancer.

He lived in Highlands virtually all his life, making his home in a modest house located in an extraordinary location at 87 Portland Road. Here, with his wife Peggy, he met and hosted old friends and new acquaintances soon to become like old friends, engaging in gentle conversation, gesturing out his picture windows to the people in town, the river and ocean he

Bahrs shortly after John and Florence Bahrs's purchase of McGuire's boathouse, rooming house and restaurant in 1917. *Courtesy Bahrs Landing.*

knew so well, his restaurant and landing by the bridge with its huge, red "Bahrs" sign, and all the Highlands he loved and called home.

"He was a terrific man, so dedicated. He always wanted to help, to do something good. He had a dynamic personality. You could have a bad day, but when you got to be around Buddy, he always cheered you up."

—Anonymous

BEAUTIFUL MEMORIES!

July 1992
Dear Ms Mullen:

When I received your former letter wherein you remark that you are receiving so many conflicting stories of "How I learned to swim in Highlands." Permit me to enlighten you. You don't mind?

But first I wish to thank you for your thoughtfulness in forwarding the pretty colorful "Invite" for the August 8th. I like it! I will place it in my huge scrapbook containing many lovely swim memories.

This Ms Mullen is the true story of how it all happened! At the age of ten my folks rented a bungalow from William Kruse that directly faced the

Shrewsbury River. All one had to do was open the front door and step onto the porch, walk a few steps to the bulkhead, step up, then leap into the river (of course, all this at high tide! Wonderful). My dad tied a rope around my waist then would lower me down into the water. This was the beginning of my swimming career! In the Shrewsbury River!

My great desire of wanting to learn the fast "American Crawl," as I then saw it, from Milton Kruse and (of Highlands) his friend John Demmertt do it as they did, after diving off the "Ole Patten Line Pier" (or dock) and swam downstream in the strong tides together to the Highlands draw bridge. For me to get a better view of them as they swam (their swim stroke) I would step down from our front porch of our cottage to the beach, at mid-tide. Then I walked along the beach, passed under Kruse's Dance Pavilion and continued over to the back of Bahrs' Restaurant. This I did to give me a safer and better view to watch Milton and John as they stroked downstream. Then I would practice what I saw them doing, and later to be told, it was a "wild stroke" (ha!). Oh, well!

You will agree that the "Ederle Park" is perfectly located, down at that part of the beach (back of Bahrs). I actually did learn to swim! And, as I was later told when joining the famous swim club, "The Women's

The most delightful photo of all, showing Pa and Ma Ederle on each side of their Trudy, with the New York City welcoming committee in the background.

Swimming Association of New York" my stroke was "wild." It needed a refined touch to join its swim team! I had a wonderful coach who had great faith in my possible abilities. He made me a perfect champion. He was the only coach who believed that the "American Crawl" could be maintained to conquer the cold, rough waters of that nasty English Channel!

Today finds every long distance swimmer using the "American Crawl." No more side strokes, breast strokes, etc. (All much too slow.) mainly for distance swims! Well it took a wonderful coach and an anxious child who loved the challenge of the seas to prove for others that there are no such words as "Can't Be Done!" The records prove it. God is good. I looked up into the heavens as I alone walked into that vast body of the English Channel on August 6, 1926. The waters cold and threatening, I said, "Please, God help me! And throughout the hours of the storm (four hours) I kept happily speaking to Him and He kept hearing me. Hat I know! It was the only way I could have succeeded, that's for sure! I finished in fine spirit! No pains and exceedingly happy! And they (everyone) said and kept telling me "It can't be done!" before the swim. It took a Yankee to show them how! The true faith of my trainer (coach) in Women's Swimming Association who was delighted to have me prove his theory of the fast American Crawl! And, not forgetting my first strokes learned on the beach of "Dear Highlands," and waters of the Shrewsbury River that "still keep rolling along." God bless it! Beautiful Memories!

These I assure you, Ms Mullen, are the true facts of ten year old Trudy Ederle's desire to swim and how God was good.!

My love to all my many dear friends in "Dear Ole Highlands!"

Gertrude Trudy Ederle
Swimmingly yours, always!

A copy of this letter was kindly given to the editor by Miss Ederle during a visit with her and her niece in Wyckoff, New Jersey.

PLAYING POLITICS IN HIGHLANDS

It's for health reasons that I am seeking retirement from politics having served the borough of Highlands since the early 1950's first as a councilman and then as mayor.

Cornelius "Neil" J. Guiney Jr. (1916–1990) has the distinction of having served the people of Highlands as mayor longer than any other person: from 1956 to 1965 and from 1974 to 1983, eighteen years.

I've learned so much about politics from the three different forms of government that we've had. Of these the one I like the best was the nonpartisan form we had from 1956 to 1974. It was outstanding, we did away with politics and we didn't have any political leader coming around asking for favors. The version of government the borough has now is and has been a disaster: you have a primary in June and in the primary everyone is fighting. Then they lay off for awhile. Then the fighting starts up again in September and goes all the way to the election. Then you don't take office until January and by the time you get around to getting all the appointed positions filled it's practically time for another primary. Politics in Highlands is ruining the town.

All we've done for the last four years is bicker. The only thing we've accomplished is to finalize plans for a river front park (the new park is expected to be completed in the summer) and it would have been done sooner if it wasn't for the bickering. There's one thing worse than politics in government and that's the Civil Service. The same group that brought politics back to Highlands is responsible for giving us the Civil Service. You can't fire anyone who isn't doing their jobs and people won't testify against anyone if you bring charges against them because they are all friends. Civil Service is fine and for big cities like Newark, Trenton or Atlantic City, but has caused us nothing but trouble. My one wish is to see the governing body make appointments on the basis of merit rather than on politics and favors. I feel sorry for whoever gets in as the next mayor. Highlands has so many things to offer more than Rumson, Fair Haven or Little Silver that are flat like Florida, with no view. We have the ocean, our river and the hills like mountains. It's really a great town. People and members of council who blame all the ills of the town on the condominiums have that all wrong. Rather than being the bane of the community's existence, the condos could change the town around. Rather than blaming the condo owners, I blame several of the borough's larger businesses: two or three of these delinquents owe approximately $75,000 in back taxes, adding greatly to the tax burden. However, I have been disappointed with the condominium owners, along with adding tax ratables to the borough's tax rolls and that's good, I had hoped that the intelligent and talented owners of these condos would become involved with town affairs. That has not happened; there's a bit of snobbishness; they're good people but they can't be bothered with politics in a small town if there is no pay. They're talented but unwilling. We need the help of everybody because when you are as divided as we are, the only people who show up at the meetings are hecklers.

Despite all this and my criticism, Highlands still is a good town. When I was first elected to council, there were no condominiums and Highlands was still a very busy place. There were boats running down from a Battery for 50¢ or $1 a passenger and it would dump the passengers off for the day. There were dance halls and lots of summer hotels and bungalows and cottages. While the town has lost its attractions over the years, it's still renowned for its great restaurants, which still draw people to our community. Of course the town has made advances with flood control projects that hopefully will spare the town of the flooding that we experienced on September 12, 1960. The aftermath of that deluge kept my insurance office busy for three months trying to settle up claims. Some things that I remember best during my political time here, one was when the town hosted Franklin Delano Roosevelt, Jr. for the 25th anniversary of the New Deal and the parade for the town's own Gertrude Ederle, the first woman to swim across the English Channel. As far as the future, I plan to rest, enjoy traveling a bit with my wife, and my biggest goal is to get my golf score back down under 100.

—Neil Guiney, 1984

WALLACE REID

Once upon a time there was a handsome young movie actor by the name of Wallace Reid. He owned the first automobile in the Highlands, bright red.

When Wallace was a young teenager he lived with his theatrical family in the house that is now the Our Lady of Perpetual Help Convent. Later the family moved to Portland Road. While living there, Wallace worked in his spare time for the Clark drug store. His parents had a busy social life and sometimes drank a bit too much. Wallace disapproved of drinking and smoking. He told Mrs. Clark that he would never do either

Handsome Highlander and Hollywood heartthrob Wallace Reid followed in the acting-writing-producing footsteps of his father, Hal Reid, and mother, Bertha Westwood, starring in more than one hundred silent films and becoming known as Hollywood's most perfect lover.

as long as he lived. One evening his parents prepared to attend a party at the Fair Haven Boat Club. Wallace thought that they were not able to drive safely. When they insisted on going, he removed a part of their car so that it would not start.

When Wallace went to Hollywood he became a star. He was handsome and had a wonderful personality. In those days serial movies were popular. For instance, a different episode would be shown every Tuesday night. The only one that I remember was the *Perils of Pauline*.

Wallace was taking part in one of these, riding on top of a railroad flat car with an actress. They were to pass through a raging fire and when they did her dress caught on fire. In trying to save her Wallace Reid was badly burned. In the hospital they gave him morphine for the pain and he became addicted which eventually caused his death. He left a wife and child. His wife wrote a book about the dangers of drugs.

—Ann McNeill

Ralph the Shoemaker

Ralph Carone was a true Highlander. He was known as "Ralph the Shoemaker." Ralph was a legend in town. You could never find a better place to get all your shoes and broken leather goods fixed. When you think of Highlands you have to think of "Ralph's Shoe Repair."

He would always put into his work unsurpassed love and talent. He was good to everybody young and old. Ralph would sew the baseball gloves for the boys and the dance shoes for the girls. He would have no problem sharing his talents and his skills with people. Sometimes he would let kids, who stopped by just to say hello, help him in little ways. No matter how many kids would be in there he never lost his temper. Ralph could always be found in his window working and he would always have a smile for you and wave. He had a very special helper who was always by his side and that was his wife Dorothy. Those two loved the customers and all their friends in Highlands. Ralph and Dorothy had three children Arnold Perry, Cathy and Robert "Bobby" Carone. Dorothy came from Highlands, too. Her maiden name was Wolcott and another large family well known in Highlands. Ralph and Dorothy have eight grandchildren, seven great-grandchildren and two great-great grandchildren.

Ralph came to Highlands in the 1930's when he was young with his father Tony Carone. Tony had opened his shoe repair shop on Valley Street. That is where Ralph learned all his shoe repair skills from his father. When Ralph was older he opened his own store on Bay Ave. Ralph's store was open six days a week. Even if the weather was bad in a blizzard or bad northeast storm, he was open and working. Even if it was after the store was officially closed or it was his day off, living behind the shop, he always opened the door to everyone. Ralph could fix just about anything. When he fixed a belt, a pair of shoes, a handbag or a baseball glove, he made it better than when it was new. He had some extraordinary skills. People would come to see Ralph from all over to have their items repaired.

When the summer people would come every year, they would bring their shoes to Ralph and he would remember everyone and all their names. It would amaze everyone that he knew exactly where everything was. He would have hundreds of shoes in his shop and he knew who owned every one of them. When you went back in to pick up your items, he knew exactly what was yours. Ralph put faces with shoes and you will never find people like that. Now days people need computers to remember stuff like he did. It was a thrill to stop and look in his windows and watch him work.

Ralph was the nicest and the most soft spoken man imaginable; he had the most loving eyes. He was a great man who would help anyone out with whatever they needed help with. When you would pick up your items, he would give you such great deals and everyone loved the sweet smell of the leather in there.

Once there was a soldier that had come into Ralph's and needed his shoes fixed. Well of course Ralph said, "Sure no problem, see you in a day or two!" Well the soldier had to return back to duty and did not return home for two years. When the soldier did return home, he went to Ralph's to see if by chance he still had his shoes. He sure did and knew exactly where they were! Ralph was an unsung hero of this great town of Highlands. Ralph was one of the best pool shooters in Highlands too. You could find him and Dorothy at the American Legion every Saturday night shooting pool. The both of them were so well known and adored in Highlands. Ralph had been in Highlands for over sixty years. He worked every day all the way up till he passed away at age 79 in 1997. Ralph was an icon in Highlands and an honest business man. This is the definition of "A True Highlander."

—Traci Perry, granddaughter of Ralph the Shoemaker

Part 8

Everyday Life Years Ago

Names

Children often have a language all their own, understood by other children only. We had our own names for places. The present Route 36 or Navesink Ave. was the "Front Road." You either went "up the road" or "down the road" depending on which direction you were heading. Highland Ave. was the "Back Road." Valley St. and Miller St. were "lanes." You either went "in the lane" or "out the lane" when you traveled on Valley St. When it came to Miller St. you were either "up" or "down" the lane.

We called Peak St. "Pig Alley" because of the number of families who lived there that raised pigs for winter feasting. The lower part of town near the river was called Parkertown for early settlers named Parker who came up from South Jersey. Most of the folks down there were clammers. I still remember the many sidewalks made of clam shells.

Our part of town was called "Irish town.""Folks on the hill above were known as "goat hillers." I remember the pigs but not any goats. Uncle Bart's family lived at the top of Miller Hill. He was grandpa's brother. They kept pigs and every fall we received a nice big piece of pork for winter time.

—Ann McNeill

STILL WORKING

In the Highlands there is still an old fashioned soda fountain. Katz's has been there for over 55 years with the same owners. Walter, Fred and Lou have seen a lot of their customers and employees grow up and get married. Katz's has a lot of great memories for me and for a lot of other people. When I was a baby I took my first steps in the store.

Every day after school I would go into Katz's and get ice cream or candy. Walter is my dad so I would go behind the counter and try to wait on customers. Sometimes the girls would let me wash the dishes and I thought that was great.

When I was 16, I started to work there. One day a clammer from South Jersey came in and after a few months we started dating. Now we are married for 10 years and I have two great sons. I still work there part-time and my sons come down to the store and help us fill the shelves and carry newspapers.

—Evelyn Clark, 2002

FRITT'S ICE CREAM PARLOR

I would like to go back to the late 1920's when I was a young boy. The town was Highlands and at that time things were booming since it was just before the Depression. The town had several soda fountains and places to buy ice cream. However, the place where most of us, young and old, met and had our favorites was a place called Fritt's ice-cream parlor and candy store.

The store was in the center of town on the main street, Bay Avenue, the location of a the United States Post Office today. Mr. Fritt, the owner, was a nice man with gray and fuzz above each year, elderly, but with all lot of pep. And the ice cream sodas were 10¢ and the marshmallow sundaes were 10¢, a ball of ice cream, marshmallow over the ice cream and a cherry on top with a glass of water, my affordable favorite. My sister's favorite was a Dusty Road, a ball of ice-cream with malted milk powder over the ice cream and a cherry for 15¢. The Banana Splits were 25¢. A large banana cut in half, three balls of ice cream, crushed pineapple, crushed strawberries and whipped cream on top.

Mr. Fritt had the patience of a saint, especially when the children were picking out penny candies. Some were two of for a penny and some were one for a penny. The decisions took a lot of time.

—William Kanovsky

Life in the Highlands 1920–1940

They were the best of times and I thought they would never end. They did, however, but the memories live on. The winters were as enjoyable as well as the summers. When one considers how we would sleigh ride down the hill on Miller St. from well above the Catholic Church all the way down to the river, tongue in cheek, and as we crossed over Highway 36, the railroad tracks and Bay Ave. In addition, there was frost fishing at the ocean and ice fishing and ice boating on the Navesink River. Along with the activities was the continual quietness of just living there.

The summers, though, were something special and included some of the following things: Waiting for the summer vacation crowd to return each year, especially the girls at the Mary Patten dock or at the train station; wearing a pair of swimming trunks all season during of the day, not wearing shoes on our feet that got so tough we could walk on broken clamshells; going fishing, crabbing, and clamming with my grandfather; attending the movies at the Highlands Marine theater; spending most of the day over at the ocean or on the river with of the girls from Williams cottages and hanging out during the night at the merry-go-round across the street or dancing at Creighton's pavilion dance hall.

On Saturday night both the permanent residents and the summer people walked down the Bay Avenue over across the old bridge to Highland Beach and back. It seemed we all knew everyone and greeted each other accordingly.

Swimming across the river to Sandy hook was a challenge and it depended upon the incoming and outgoing tide. The tide was swift and you could not swim directly across. You had to swim downstream or upstream. The end was unpredictable. In addition, diving off the Highlands bridge when no one was looking and skinny dipping were in vogue.

When we grew older Conners, Bahrs, Ahearns and the Bamboo Room were the places to go on a Saturday night to meet friends, drink a few beers and dance the night away.

My family in the Highlands included my grandparents, William and Carrie Weber, who lived on Valley Street in the heart of Parkertown. My grandfather was in the of the lobster business before becoming the custodian of Highlands Elementary School. My grandmother was a friend of Jennie Parker, often referred to as Aunt Jennie of Parkertown. She lived down the street. My aunt Gertrude Weber Johnson was a friend of Gertrude Ederle and used to row the boat when Ederle practiced for her English Channel swim. Dr. John L. Offerman was my doctor. The Highlands in my day was somewhat like living in Camelot. The days were fun and endless and the residents were the best.

—Thomas Weber, January 8, 2000

Growing Up in Highlands

In 1950, four years into his American experience, my father bought a business in Highlands. The property he bought (for less than the price of a 1999 Geo Metro) consisted of a main street hardware store with inventory, two apartments—one bathroom between them—above, and a large stable building in the back, with two apartments above that. We lived in one of the apartments above the store. It soon became obvious that sharing a bathroom with another family just wouldn't work out, so for most of the ten years we lived there, the front apartment was furnished, but vacant.

A hurricane hit in December, 1950, making Bay Ave. indistinguishable from the bay itself. The damage was extensive and the town never really recovered from that flood and the next one that came three years later and ended all hope of renewal.

Highlands had three hardware stores to serve a year-round population of about three thousand. But that wasn't nearly as dismal as another statistic—it also had 23 taverns, which was understandable when it had a summer population increase, but when there were no more visitors, the town had a depressing number of closed cocktail lounges.

With the floods threatening to wash us away, my mother took advantage of my attention being diverted, and snuck off to Newark to buy me a baby brother. He increased the population of Jews in Highlands by about 10%. When he entered school he doubled the Jewish population at the school. The two other Jewish families in town—the Cohens, who owned a small grocery and the Katzes, who owned first a candy store and then a luncheonette—had no children in school.

Where I learned about the three R's was Highlands Grammar School. There was one classroom for each grade and each teacher was at least 65 years old. My kindergarten teacher, Miss O'Neal, before she was forced to retire, had taught for 65 years! Being the only Jews in school had its disadvantages, but it also had advantages, too.

In fifth grade I was a proud member of that elite corps of paramilitary officers, the Safety Patrol. One of my tasks was to accompany home the children from morning kindergarten and then return to school. Sometimes I forgot to return to school for the afternoon, on days when my mother wasn't home. A couple of times I stayed home all day and told the attendance officers the next day that it had been a Jewish holiday. I was always beyond suspicion, and the fact that my brother had been in school on this supposed Jewish holiday was never brought up.

My public school classmates were not exactly disciples of diversity. In the McCathy era, those from eastern Europe were all considered "Russians" who were all Communists looking to brainwash others to be the same. Jews were not Americans.

One Spring day in 1960, I awoke to a smell of smoke. A fire did extensive damage to our home. My most cogent memory of the day is how disappointed I was that I would have to go to school that day. My parents simply refused to recognize the well-known principle that a house burning down was a good enough reason to miss school. The house was torn down, after the property was purchased by the Borough of Highlands, and is now the site of the Highlands Fire Dept.

Whenever I get a chance I go back to check the place out. It is a town that was once a desirable recreation destination. It was served by a train line. It had a wonderful merry-go-round. It was a terrific place for my Newark relatives to come to, and enjoy its safe sandy beaches. All in all, except for the fact that they made me go to school, it was a pretty good place to grow up in.

—Paul Klein

At Home in the Lighthouse

Hello and welcome to my home in the Twin Lights. I am Elsie Jane Rockette Horan, the daughter of Murphy Lee Rockette, the last

Twin Lights' last lighthouse keeper, from 1921 to 1952, was Murphy Rockette, standing before the great Fresnel lens of the south tower in 1939.

lighthouse keeper there and these are some of my memories up there on the hill living under the lights. Everyone used to call my home Twin Lights, but the official name was Navesink Light Station. It was the site of many important historical events but for me and my sister, Virginia Rockette Gowers, it was just a wonderful place to grow up.

My dad had been in the army and navy for some twelve years and even had some college before sitting for the U.S. Lighthouse Service examination in 1921. Mom proudly told us that his score was so high that he was allowed to choose his assignment. Mom insisted on living on land, not some isolated crag in the sea, so Twin Lights became home for the Rockette family for more than thirty years.

On the right side of the vestibule here we had an African Grey Parrot. The parrot used to whistle to all the girls going by and to the ladies that would come to visit the Twin Lights. Entering the kitchen on the left was a long handled pump to pump water. At first there was no electricity and kerosene lamps provided illumination for cooking and reading. Just think, no light in the lighthouse! There was no plumbing in the quarters for quite some time. Outside there were two outhouses across the paved road by the clothes line area. Here we kept a pet goat named Nancy. Kids from school were a bit jealous; they had dogs and cats, but we had a parrot and a goat.

I remember the big black cooking stove in the kitchen which my mother, Elsie, used to polish once a week with black polish to make it shine. The kitchen was the heart of the home; it was always warm and inviting, especially in winter when frigid northeast stormy winds blasted the lighthouse. Everything had to be spotless. The head Superintendent of Lighthouses used to come Staten Island to inspect and give everything the white glove inspection and grade my father on the findings; he even came into our family rooms, expecting everything to be neat and tidy. A single smudge or fingerprint found on the big Fresnel lens was cause for rejection.

Dad's rocking chair was in the far corner of the kitchen, where after a hard day he would relax and smoke his pipe.

My sister and I shared the bedroom at the top of the stairs. I loved it, as I could look out the window and view the Navesink River, Atlantic Ocean, and the entrance to New York Harbor. The Ambrose and Sandy Hook Lightships used to blink off and on all night there in the ocean. Of course, I could see the light flashing from the big Fresnel lens at night out my window. It was breathtaking. It was just something else. We used to joke that our Dad always left the light on for us. In day time we were awed by the vista, especially on clear crisp days in September and October, when we could see as far as lower Manhattan and the Empire State Building. We liked to see all the big cargo and passenger steam ships coming and going, dreaming about distant lands they were headed to or from.

My sister, Virginia Lee, was four years old when our dad was stationed here in 1921, so we had a dozen years difference in ages. He was a lighthouse keeper for 31 years and retired in 1952. The bedroom facing the wooded area was my parents' room where I was born September 1, 1929.

Twin Lights, with only the north tower showing, celebrates its 150th anniversary this year. One of the second-floor windows was in the room Virginia and Elsie Jane Rockette shared as they grew up "under the lights."

They had a midwife in Highlands. Her name was Aunt Jennie and she helped the birth of half the children in town. She didn't work for any doctor. We had Dr. Opfermann, his office was right above Bedle's Drug Store on Miller St. Opfermann came up, but Aunt Jennie would really take over until she actually needed the doctor. Jennie Parker was her name and, in fact, the Jennie Parker Manor down there, next to the school, those apartment houses were named after her. I know my dad went down and got her and brought her up here. There was no going to a hospital in those days.

Virginia, Ginny, was of course always like a big sister to me and despite our ages we shared precious time growing up. It was always Ginny and E.J. together as much as possible. We read, played games like cards and pick-up sticks, and board games, and listened to the radio—great reception being two hundred feet above sea level in view of all the New York City stations. School and friends kept us busy and in winter when it snowed and cars could not make it up the steep hill, we pulled a sled of groceries from the A&P on Bay Avenue two hundred feet up hill. Of course, the snow gave us the best sleigh rides of any kid and at great speeds, about a mile long, down to Miller St. and beyond to the river.

—Elsie Jane "E.J." (Rockette) Horan

Hillside Springs

Lots of the summer and year-round people in the Highlands back in the 1950's preferred spring water more than the stuff coming from the town's water supply.

When you would open the tap in our bungalow's kitchen for a glass of water, it came out white like milk due to the great amount of air dissolved in the water. Despite this the water was perfectly good, though somewhat fizzy, as it came up from the deep underground artesian wells located on Miller Street just below the clothing factory and you had to wait and let the water stand for awhile until the air in it is escaped and it cleared.

Every couple of days each summer my mother would send me off with a folding shopping cart and six or eight glass jugs to get fresh spring water from the hillside tap near the water pumping plant. There used to be a wooden trough or box into which the water constantly flowed with no way to shut it off. There were always a couple of cups or glasses on the edge of the trough for anyone who was thirsty to use. Nobody was concerned about germs back then! There used to be another source of spring water flowing from the hillside over in Water Witch near Hollywood's place.

The hillside spring water was the best and also the coldest and how it hurt your teeth when you bent over and drank right from the pipe!

—Jim Grazide, 1996

Our Well

When I was growing up we had a well. It contained the sweetest, coldest water I ever tasted. I was not the only one who cherished it. All kinds of workmen passing by in their wagons would stop long enough for a drink to cool themselves off. A pail and a dipper were always ready on a bench.

The taste and quality of the water was due in a large part to the fact that the well was lined with stone from the old lighthouse at Twin Lights. It is recorded that the lighthouse was built in 1828 of good blue split stone at a cost of $8,440. It was probably demolished in 1862 and grandpa somehow, through the Hartshornes, got some of the stones.

—Ann McNeill

The Ice Business in Highlands

My husband, Roy Maxson, and his father, Burt Maxson, started an ice business. In the summertime. What year? Well, it was in being, here, when I arrived here, and that was before 1930. Sometime in the late '20s. Anyhow, when they weren't out clamming on the river, they had an ice business. At that time, my husband, Roy, before they started their own business, had worked for Seaboard Ice Company. And by the time that his father was starting his own business he needed a lot of help. When Roy went to work on his route for Seaboard, he was helping his father out and of course that did not go well with Seaboard because when Roy would help his father, that would drag a lot of customers away from Seaboard Ice and Coal Company. So finally they had to tell Roy, he had either to work for them or work for his father. So he chose to work for his father. And they only had two trucks at that time. Roy had one and his father had one. Eventually they were able to get most of the Seaboard business away. We had all the bungalows in Conners. We had all of them on the Fifth Street. We had all the bungalows in the, uh, in the grove up there, I forget. Well I can't remember it, anyhow there was a grove there. Well it had about forty... To make matters short we had about all of the summer business. We had Conners. I think Conners had about forty-two bungalows. And they also had the hotel. Conners hotel. And a guy named Blackie, you know his name was Black, the father of all these Black boys, Herman his name was. He wanted my husband, Roy, to give him ice free for the hotel because he had all the bungalows. And your grandfather told him to go to hell. He said, "I don't need this kind of business." And he said, "Well, if you don't come in here and give me my ice free for the hotel, you can't come in and serve my bungalows." And your grandfather said to him, "That's what you think." So he went and talked to Marie Black who really owned it all. Her husband didn't own nothing. Her father left it to her. And she said, "I tell you what, Roy, you still have all the bungalows. And besides, the bungalows wouldn't have anyone else but you." She said, "They go to the beach. They leave their doors open. You know how much they're going to need and they're well satisfied that you ain't going to jimmie them for more than they need. And if you think I'm going to let him do that, no." So they built it up and up, the business that when my husband's brother Percy was old enough to get a license, he had a truck, okay. You never realized any profits until after the 4th of July. The name of the company was the Independent Ice Company. We employed four other men to work with Pop, that is Burt, and Roy and Percy. When my brother got old enough, he came down to work, William Tierney, to work for us in the summer. And he was Pop's help. Naturally, Pop had all the taverns. We only had thirty-three of them in those days and I think Pop served most all of them for Independent. They would pull up to a tavern. Then you had to chop the ice to take it into the taverns to put on the coolers. That's the way they kept it cold, with chopped ice. Well, brother would chop the ice, and chop and chop and chop and take it in, and Pop would be sitting at the bar. And when it came time at the end of the week to pay up for the ice, you know Pop never had any profits. He drank the ice away just like he drank the clams away. Then one time we had an ice house on Miller street where we stored the ice. Bubbie, my brother would load up the ice on the truck and all. He says, "Pop don't forget to close the rear of the truck." They started up Miller hill, and what do you think, that is right, all the ice slides out onto the street.

The business started to depreciate right at the end of the war in '46 and '47. The mass production refrigerators that manufactured the ice. So from the late '20s to '46–47 we had the ice every summer.

—Lillian Maxson, from an interview by David Maxson, 1996

Winters

Winters in by-gone days were not always pleasant even for a child. It was a daily battle just to keep warm. We had three stoves: one big black one in the kitchen and two tall thin ones for the dining room and the parlor. The two thin ones were taken down each spring and stored away in the summer kitchen. They were brought out again in the fall. The one in the parlor was lit only on rare occasions. The door to that room was kept closed.

Coal was delivered by the ton. The man who delivered it carried twenty bags on his back, from the road, and dumped it down a chute into the cellar. All of that coal was hauled upstairs in a coal scuttle as it was needed. Wood was delivered in short pieces and stored in the barn. Later it had to be split with an ax or hatchet. That was hard work for a woman.

I bathed in a brown and white bath tub in front of the kitchen stove. I also undressed there. Before I went to bed mother heated a flat iron, rolled it in one of her gingham aprons and put it at the foot of my bed. Often when I awoke I found the water in the hall pitcher frozen.

—Ann McNeill

Food Shopping

Meat

Before my time and before there were butcher stores in the Highlands, a butcher with a horse and wagon came by and supplied my family with meat. In my early years, a Mr. Teaney kept a butcher shop down near the bridge. It was almost a mile walk to buy meat.

Our back yard looked different then. A chicken house stood where the garage is now. Across the driveway was a barn where Uncle [James W. McGarry], a road overseer, kept his horses. Connecting the barn and the house was a shed where Grandma kept one or two cows. They supplied milk and butter until they were sold to the butcher. The shed also covered the outhouse. I personally do not remember the shed but the chicken house and barn were there for a good part of my life. The upper part of the barn, which used to be the hay loft, was in my time a playhouse for me and my friends. In the two stalls below there were always kittens. Thank goodness there was always someone to adopt an extra kitten. The barn was demolished in 1949 by Jess (Jordan) and his father. Some of that lumber ended up as part of the garage and the upstairs floor boards in the Jordan residence [273 Chapel Hill Road, Middletown].

Another butcher was Otto Gautchy. He had two daughters, Helen and Marie. At our September, 1990 meeting of the Needlework Guild [at King James Care Center] I discovered that one of our new members was Helen, now Helen Higgins.

Summer Vegetables

When we stopped planting a garden we depended on Mr. Jake Linzmayer from Atlantic Highlands to supply us with fruits and vegetables. Twice a week he drove his wagon down to the Highlands and stopped at every house. His wagon was a delight to behold. So colorful! Sometimes he would let me climb on the back step to get a better view or pick out a perfect piece of fruit.

Over the years I have viewed many a supermarket with its bins and bins of fruits and vegetables, but never have I experienced the pleasure I felt when Mr. Linzmayer's wagon pulled up at our front gate.

Winter Vegetables

Every fall a farmer from around Vandenburg, called Mr. Campbell, stopped by to get our order for winter vegetables. We bought potatoes by the barrel. I believe they were one dollar a barrel back then. We ordered potatoes, turnips, carrots, cabbage and pumpkins. A couple of weeks later Mr. Campbell would return with his son, Clarence, to deliver our order. These things were stored in the root cellar. When spring came around the remaining potatoes would have sprouted and I would be sent down to the cellar to "snag" them. That was definitely not my favorite task!

It was at 35 Miller Street that John and Angelina Azzolina, from close-by Sicilian towns, opened their candy-grocery-butcher shop, living behind and above the store, always ready to help and serve Highlanders. Here son Joe learned the food trade and, after World War II, returned home and convinced his father to start up the Highlands Food Basket, at 123 Bay Avenue, now Grimaldi's Pizzeria.

Shopping in New York

Twice a year Auntie and I went to New York on the boat to order supplies. We went to a big warehouse on Vessey St. named Callahan and Kemp. Our order was not always the same. Sometimes it would be a barrel of flour, a half barrel of sugar, a half tub of butter, a couple of sides of bacon and always ten pounds of broken cookies for me. They were cheaper that way and tasted just as good. We also got a big tin box of coffee and one of tea. The tops were hinged and the boxes must have held at least ten pounds each. Back home the same day, I would be sent down the next morning to tell the express man that we were expecting things on the boat and ask him to deliver them to us. When the things arrived the flour and sugar were stored in the summer kitchen. The tea, coffee, and cookies went into the kitchen cupboard and the salted butter in the basement where it kept beautifully.

—Ann McNeill

OUR START IN HIGHLANDS

Joe Azzolina grew up in Highlands, and he never forgot his home town, returning frequently for special events and ceremonies like the Highlands 100th anniversary party at Bahrs in 2000.

We started out in the grocery business in Highlands, at number 35 Miller St. That was 75 years ago. My parents moved to Highlands when I was a baby and invested $2,000 in a candy store, which was a considerable amount of money for the time but they felt they could make a go of it, as they knew Highlands from summer visits. They lived in Newark where my father was in the jewelry business. Both my parents, Joseph and Angelina Azzolina, were from nearby villages in Sicily. At first my mother ran the candy store and my father commuted on the trains to his job, but then the business began to grow rapidly and he worked the store full time, cutting meat, stocking shelves, waiting on customers. They got a good reputation with Highlanders, especially the clammers and their families; they were thoughtful and kind and generous with credit. They often opened for customers after hours, if someone needed a quarter-pound of butter or something. We lived right there behind the store and later above it. My sister Grace and I also worked and went to school at the same time. We used to deliver groceries throughout town in a small wagon.

During the Depression the years were lean but fun and we got by and helped Highlands families cope as well. My father used the barter system and kept track of charges families ran up under mouse traps. Hard work and diligence kept the business going and doing well.

—Joe Azzolina

High School

1910–1914

In September 1910 a class of over sixty freshmen gathered at Atlantic Highlands. They came from Middletown Township, Highlands, and Atlantic Highlands and represented many grammar schools. We were to become a very close unit. Our classroom teacher was Miss Wall, a quiet lady but strict. The very first day she sent Victor Grossinger and me to the office for whispering. We were both good kids and it scared us to death. Victor headed for the basement but I went as far as the office. The door was ajar and when I saw Professor Cossaboom sitting at his desk and looking so stern, I too fled to the basement. We returned for the next class and nothing was said.

At that time no colored families lived in the Highlands so I was fascinated by the four colored girls who sat opposite from me and we became good friends. Two names have faded from memory; the other two were Mary Mitchell and Bessie Robinson. Years later I met Mary in Red Bank and received a big hug and an introduction to her grown daughter. Bessie was a minister's daughter. She made me laugh. She made up jokes and jingles. One I remember was "Lord bless us / Get behind us / Throw us in a ditch / So Miss Wall can't find us."

That was a glorious year, but next fall all of Middletown Township pupils were sent to the old Andrews Hotel in Navesink. We were devastated. We had an hour and a half for lunch so often we would grab our lunch and head for Andrews Hotel to spend a few minutes with our friends. The following year Leonardo High School was finished; the Middletown Township students went there and we lost track. In 1914 the first class to graduate from Leonardo High was part of our class. I don't know how many were in that graduating class. I have heard that there were ten. One of them, Gladys Coe, now lives on a farm outside Princeton with her son. When my class graduated from Atlantic Highlands High School there were six of us. I was Valedictorian and am the lone survivor.

—Ann McNeill

Taking the Train to School

Highlands kids used to take the train to High School. When I was the agent in the Highlands, I would sell tickets every month. The students would pick up their tickets. I had a list, and the Board of Education would cut me a voucher to pay for the student tickets. I think they were $4 per person per month. And when they did away with the trains and put the busses on, they charged $10 a month. Some students got off in Atlantic Highlands and walked to the school on First Ave. Others got off at Leonardo Station and walked up to the school on Leonardville Rd. at Hosford's Ave.

—G. Lester Whitfield

College

When I made plans to go to college in Trenton another Highlands girl decided to go also. Although we weren't close friends, we roomed together, first in the Annex, later in the main building. We came home only twice a year, Christmas and Easter. We traveled by trolley. It took us four hours and cost one dollar. We took the Fast Line to Trenton Junction. There we got a trolley to South Amboy. At South Amboy we caught a trolley to Campbell's Junction. There we finally got a trolley which took us home. By that time our suitcases weighed a ton. Our laundry was mailed home and mailed back again. Whenever a box of goodies arrived from home we were sure to have a bunch of visitors that evening.

—Ann McNeill

Swamp Willow

In Swamp Willow, *by Edwina Elroy, the setting is the hills, the river, the bay and ocean of Highlands. The characters are real Highlanders, if not in person then at least in spirit and style of life; they live on the water and by the water as clammers, lobstermen or rumrunners, being true watermen. And as Highlanders and always independent, they support themselves through hard work and untaught skills and care for their families and friends around town when the need is known. They treat outsiders with tolerance and a degree of mistrust. Highlanders who happen to leave the waters and hills, either by choice or by necessity, in time feel compelled to return to continue life by the river, either in person or in the imagination and memories of the heart. All this and more is to be found in* Swamp Willow.

Advertisement in the Local Newspaper

This is the story of Tannertown just down the river from Red Bank, a distance made long by way of life. In particular it is the story of Holly Tanner and the men who filled her life—Big Lem, her father, who raised her among the shacks and shanties of the lobstermen; Kirk who always loved her but went away; Sid who betrayed her; Ben who protected her; and Larry Ainsworth, the handsome wanderer, who tempted her to leave the waterfront she loved. $8.00

The reaction of people about town to the novel was not initially approving, either because it portrayed the community in less than positive terms or because far too many individuals identified themselves, their friends and their relatives—or thought they did—with the characters and actions of the story, and this threatened and disturbed them.

Selections from Swamp Willow

The Town

Rivenhill leans upon the river, and the river upon the sea. On its short twenty-mile journey from the Bay to the reed and cattail terminus beyond Red Bank, the river passes many towns, yet only one embraces it sensuously. Other towns have built away from the vagaries of the tidewater. Rivenhill alone lays its body brazenly against the tides.

There are also the hills whose shadow falls upon the river and which share with it the creation of the town. Their soil is copper-hued, their summits crowned with woodlands. They are hills with the dignity of mountains, and they form a western bastion against the farm country of Monmouth County, whose pastoral pattern because of them has never been woven into the tapestry of the town.

In the late nineteenth century the era of race tracks and gambling that spurred the growth of many north Jersey resorts, Rivenhill was divided into four parts: Tannertown beside the marshes, whose acres of plume grass hide sweet secret waterways and the nestings of cranes and clappers, the haunts of kingfishers and red-winged blackbirds; Sand Street, a belt of trade with middle class houses at one end and Station Square at the other; Quality Hill, the high-water mark of Rivenhill's expansion, top heavy with late Victorian architecture; the Estates on higher hills, in deeper wooded summits. Long after its decay these sections remained the divisions of Rivenhill's caste system.

Consider particularly the river people who live north of the big ditch in Tannertown. Consider them because they are the town. Their ancestors were the early squatters who crowded the peaceful Shongo Indians from their fishing grounds. Their laughter drifts over the Big Ditch into Sand Street to tantalize the burghers. No monochrome of commerce can dim their color, no effort of gentility hush their mirth. They wear their badge of bastardy with exuberance and they wait. Time is their ally. Time, and the swarms of children born with and without the benefit of clergy.

Between the hilltops and the riverfront there are affinities—love for the golden Jersey soil and for the tidal river and for the sea beyond the Hook. As

The village of Parkertown as seen from Twin Lights, circa 1910, just before the town expanded with the reclamation of the swampy lands on the right by pumping and spreading sand from the river.

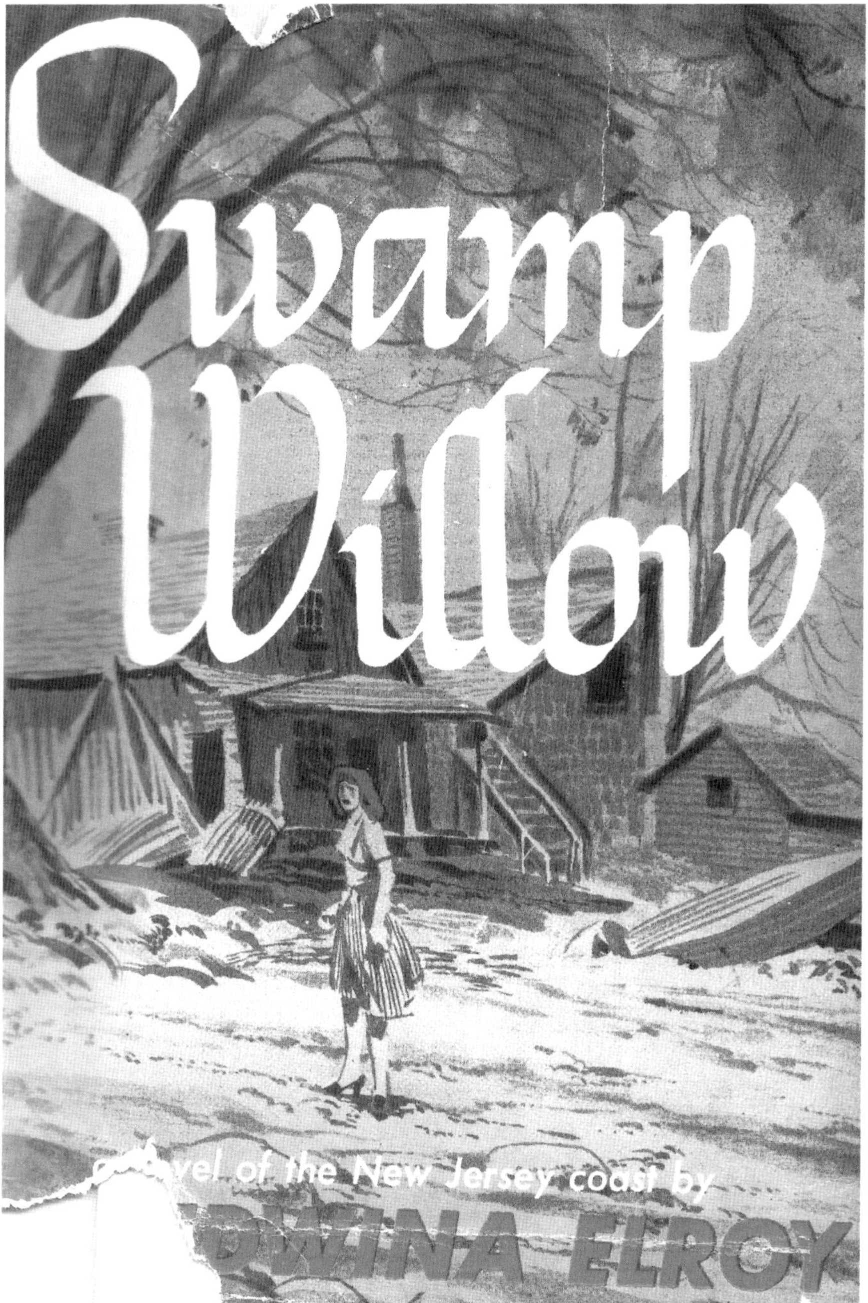

From the editor's collection, a rare, if weathered and torn, dust jacket from the hard-to-find novel *Swamp Willow*. The hard-backed novel was later reprinted as a 35 cent Harlequin Book, featuring "water front life, brawling sailors, rum-runners, and Holly Tanner."

long as the squatters have lived by the marshes a few wealthy families have lived in the hills on their vast properties whose grants for the most part bear colonial dates.

Given time, the estates, too, will pass away. The river people of Tannertown will never pass away. They will survive as long as the Atlantic feeds the river and the hills stand to the west.

Highlands is Home

I got a cousin Sam. He told me onct, he said, "Us Tanners can't live away from the river." I thought he was soft-headed. I had to come to Chicago to find out Sam was right.

Holly thought about that "something in your mind." She said, "It's like Rivenhill, most like. People think Rivenhill is just a town on a river, Old Sid, he always calls it a mudhole. I had to get far away, far as Chicago, 'fore I knowed that Rivenhill was everythin' I wanted."

Swamp Willow

The sun was breaking through the overcast and shedding a liquid loveliness upon the hills whose shadow fell upon the river, and upon the town it cast a glow, upon her town that laid its body brazenly against the tides. She turned her boat for Tanner's Cove. As Holly drew near to the land, she saw it, the swamp willow that stood and grew in ragged loneliness by the river's edge.

"See that tree?" She patted the great bole of the willow…"I'm like this tree. My roots go way down deep and I'm here t' stay."

—*Swamp Willow* by Edwina Elroy
(New York: G.P. Putnam's Sons, 1947)

Part 9

Miscellaneous Highlands Memories

View from the Back Seat

In 1927 I went to Newark State Normal School and the first week the geography teacher asked the class what was the highest point on the Atlantic Coast. She got no response. The she looked at me and a girl from Red Bank and said that we certainly should know. But she still drew a blank. How was I to know that Mount Mitchill was famous? I only knew as a teenager that it was a great place to see a scenic view if we could only find a boy with a car and it was much better at night. Then you could see the lights of Coney Island with a little smooching thrown in.

—Elizabeth S. Smith

Helping Find Our Way

I can remember going to church on Sunday evening and perhaps there'd be six or eight people there. And my old girlfriend would be sitting in one corner and I would be over in the other and I always remember Mr. Marshall. He ran the Marshall House. Even though he didn't have much dough, he would always put a dollar in the box, the collection plate. That impressed me a bit, because in those days, other than those who were in the racket of getting booze, no one had very much. Times were tough.

I remember on New Year's Eve we'd go to the service to celebrate the years going in and coming out. It was an impressive service with the candlelight and everything like this. And of course we were young kids and it was very important to go to church on New Year's Eve. To welcome in the new year with a new faith, a new hope, a new grip on life. To try to help us to tell us where we were going. None of us knew where we were heading. We were there, we were hoping, we were thinking but it was sort of a religious thing that maybe we could, in this turmoil of life, that we could be singled out somehow or somewhere, that maybe we could make a go of it. Whether you were going to be digging clams, or catching bait, skinning eels, catching fish, or whatever. We always had the hope that sometime tomorrow, instead of getting a hundred worms when digging we'd get two hundred. We always had the hope. Well fortunately for me and my brothers it worked out all right. Thank God.

—John A. Bahrs, 1996

Mass in the 1860s

Before Red Bank had a Catholic church, priests came down from Newark to minister to Catholics there. About 1864 the priests extended their mission to the Highlands. Whenever possible a priest would ride over from Red Bank on horseback, in a buggy, or on the steamboat. He would arrive on Saturday evening, stay at our house all night and celebrate Mass in the morning there in the house.

Grandpa [James McGarry] was a Catholic; grandma [Anne Hayes] was an Episcopalian, but died as a Catholic. They were married in an Episcopal church in New York. Some of the early Catholic families at that time were Grady, Reardon, Brennan, Hance, Fleming, Drinnen, and, of course, McGarry. Others were Martin, Horan, Farrell, Fay, Welsh, McIntire, Creighton, McGuire and Rowland.

When the congregation got too big for a house, services were moved to the little schoolhouse on South Peak St. in 1877. Now it's called Grand Tour, at number 46. Grandpa carried coal all the way up there and Grandma made the Communion bread from flour and water baked between flat irons. Later something like a waffle iron was used. It had one big circle in the center for the large wafer for the priest and smaller ones around it. This, the chalice and patens were stored in the corner cupboard of our living room until St. Agnes in Atlantic Highlands was built in 1891 and they were taken there.

—Ann McNeill

The Victory Clock

Well, you see, here's another part of the story during bootlegging times. We were living in the houseboat and rough times like that. Rev. Domenic Graham was the pastor of the Methodist church and he wore a big black coat. It was his job every Monday morning to walk through town, along Bay Ave., down Miller and then Fourth and Fifth streets and stop at every tavern, gin mill, speakeasy, whatever, to make collections. He was a very fine looking man. He'd just walk down and hit every place, put his hat on the table and ask if anyone needed pastoral care during such illegal and violent times. All the thieves and all the guys who were in this operation would give some dough. Of course, the church prospered and we got a new clock in the church bell and clock tower that had a big gaping hole since 1908 when the church went up. People associated the clock with the soldiers monument at the bridge and the victory in World War One and so it became the Victory clock. That was 1922 or so.

—John A. Bahrs

My Family and the Highlands

I remember growing up I used to listen to all kinds of stories told about life in times past. That kind of talk was a major recreational activity, it seems, of my old Irish grandmother, my mother, and my two aunts. I think I probably enjoyed their stories almost as much as the treat of listening to ancient songs and vaudeville routines on the old crank up Victrola record player in the corner of my grandmother's "front room."

I recall how the town was spoken of, and it seemed pretty strange to me. They all called what I knew only as Highlands "the Highlands." What's more they spoke of "the Atlantic Highlands" as well. And, Campbell's Junction they called "the Junction." As a kid I often wondered what a junction was,

The *Mary K.* at Highlands, circa 1910, with her captain, Thomas King, and wife, Mary, and boys Barney, Joey and Eddie and their girlfriends. Youngest son, John Patrick, is seen with his head stuck in the porthole and requiring a blacksmith's skills to free him.

but, of course, I never questioned any of this. I knew better. They liked children who were listeners. So I listened and filed it all away, little knowing that almost fifty years later much of that stuff would be important to me as a Highlands history writer.

They used to speak about leaving the city, i.e., New York's lower east side just above the Brooklyn bridge (and wasn't it a grand place to live!) and coming down to either Leonardo or the Highlands. They took the steamboats, the *Mandalay* for Leonardo, getting off the pier in Atlantic Highlands and taking a jitney to the cottage (now long gone after the Navy Pier came in and erased the community there) or even walking the two miles of dirt roads. If they went to the Highlands they took either the *Mandalay* and walked, jitneyed or trained or they would simply take a steamboat of either the Patten Line or the Red Bank line and get off at the Highlands. They probably also took the Sandy Hook Boats to the pier in Atlantic Highlands and then a train to Leonardo; yet they never mentioned it.

I remember my mother telling how she and one or two of her sisters, Winnie or Mary, might spend a day or part of an evening in the Highlands. There were things to do there, whereas in Leonardo it was total isolated relaxation. She remembered how she had had her picture taken with some cousins, posed in front of a scenic backdrop of the Highlands hills. She would find that picture sometime and show it me, she said. She never did. She mentioned, maybe once or twice, that she and my father had met there in Highlands, or more correctly, on the steamboat coming over from Manhattan, and that there was a postcard I should see written by my father to my Grandma King. But she did not have it and maybe she would ask my Aunt Helen about it.

My mother spoke of how grand it was, times in Highlands, with so many things to do and so close to New York. My grandma and my aunts, of course, agreed. They used to speak of how my Grandpa King had a leather horse harness business on Canal St. in New York, and they figured he had a bit of money and so had bought a boat to take the family out on excursions. Of course, one of the places on his navigation chart was the Highlands, coming either from Jersey City or Manhattan, for he had homes in both places at different times. The boat was called the *Mary K.*, named after my Grandma, Mary King. It had a big shiny brass bell with "Mary K." engraved on it. And this my Aunt Helen had in her garage or cellar. There was a picture of the boat, not black and white, but sepia toned and looking very ancient to me, and frequently my mother would take it out of the big tin box she kept her important papers in and show it around. She always pointed out my Grandmother and Grandfather, Thomas King, reminding me that my brother was named after him and that Uncle Barney, in the picture, was actually named Thomas Bernard, also after him as the first born. She never failed to point out and I never failed to delight in the figure of my father, John Patrick King. It seems he had heard a photograph, a professional photograph, was going to be taken of the boat, moored along the steamboat dock by Creighton's where the photo gallery was located, and all the people on deck. My father, a mere boy of 10 years, had been sent below and told to stay out of the way, however. He was obviously determined to be in the picture and so he opened the porthole and stuck his head out. There his head remained, stuck for good! His tears had no effect. No amount of lard would help, either. They had to call a blacksmith to unscrew the brass frame and cut it off my father's neck. Again his tears had no effect in stopping the good beating his rump received.

Many pictures were loaned or given me when I was doing the Images of America Arcadia book, *The Highlands*, back in 1995. I reviewed them all closely. Imagine the thrill and surprise when I carefully examined a photograph with a strong lens. There hanging on the cottage post was a life saving ring with the words "Mary K.," from my Grandpa's boat! I rushed it to my Aunt Helen who named several of the people seated before the porch. She wasn't there, or at least could not be seen, since she was a baby still inside my Grandma's belly at that time. Another photograph I borrowed showed my Grandpa, Thomas King, and his family on the sand and wooden boardwalks in front of their cottage, rented for the entire summer, in Tom McGuiness's Grove.

—John P. King, July 14, 2002

The Old Cemetery

Well, I can't say how old your house [of John and Helen King, 254 Navesink Avenue] might be. But I remember often walking past it four times a day on my way to and from the grammar school. Children went home for lunch back then. School used to be on Navesink Avenue across from the Catholic church until the school burned down. That was 1928. And I am eighty-six years old. I was in the first grade. I am certain of that.

You see, I remember hearing they were digging up the graves at the old Dutch church at Fifth and Valley. Just behind Jennie Parker's house.

The Reformed Church, the first church in Highlands, dated to 1875, founded by Reverend Abraham Allen. The small graveyard was behind the fence to the right. It became the Episcopal church of St. Andrew the Apostle until 1914.

All Saints Memorial Episcopal Church in Navesink, itself a registered historic site commonly known as Stone Church, welcomed the opportunity to find and memorialize the old Highlands burials.

Through the generosity of the pastor and the National Landmark Trust of All Saints Memorial Episcopal Church, soil-penetrating radar found the site where the Highlands bodies were reburied so this memorial marker could be erected and dedicated on April 15, 2007. The names of only four persons interred here are yet known. The earliest grave may date to 1876.

When the school dismissal bell rang, we bolted out and down the hill to see it. That was 1914. St. Andrew's was selling the property, and the graves had to be removed. They reburied about a dozen in the Stone Church cemetery. I remember seeing them in a circle, with a cross in the center, which had fallen over.

You know, your house was "the hospital." Old Highlanders call it that. A Dr. Mary Reed ran a baby hospital there for a number of years. Lots of babies were born there.

—Estelle White, from an interview in August 1993 by John P. King

THE BABY HOSPITAL

Referring to the Dr. Mary Reed Maternity Hospital on Navesink Ave., and I don't know if any of you folks here was born there or not but they had three rooms upstairs and two mothers in each one, one was blue, one green, and a yellow room. Once at one time she had so many mothers that she had two in the garage out back (It was summer time, of course.) and two in the front parlor. And they used to come in and there was no such thing as putting down the money up front, you know and many a time she got stuck without, you know, them paying. She was the best, Dr. Mary Reed, and I worked for her, in taking the baby from the doctor and I never saw anybody as good as she was in delivering babies. Now that's the truth. She had to close 'cause she couldn't make a go of it in the Depression, and they made the house into a rooming, a boarding house. Hard times they were then. People did not have money to pay the full bill. Sometimes they brought Dr. Mary clams, or crabs, and corn, even clam chowder. They honestly did what they could, but Dr. Mary had bills to pay in cash, not clams.

Dr. Reed lived right there on the third floor with the women and babies and her aunt used to do the cooking and they used to have regular meals there. She had a regular up-to-date and sparkling room for deliveries, with a special table, a sink, scales, and such. That was in the back, second floor. Up front she had a little room fixed up as a nursery, with big windows for summer cool and a radiator to keep the babies warm in winter. They did not sleep with their mothers, of course, but were brought to them for nursing (my job, day and night).

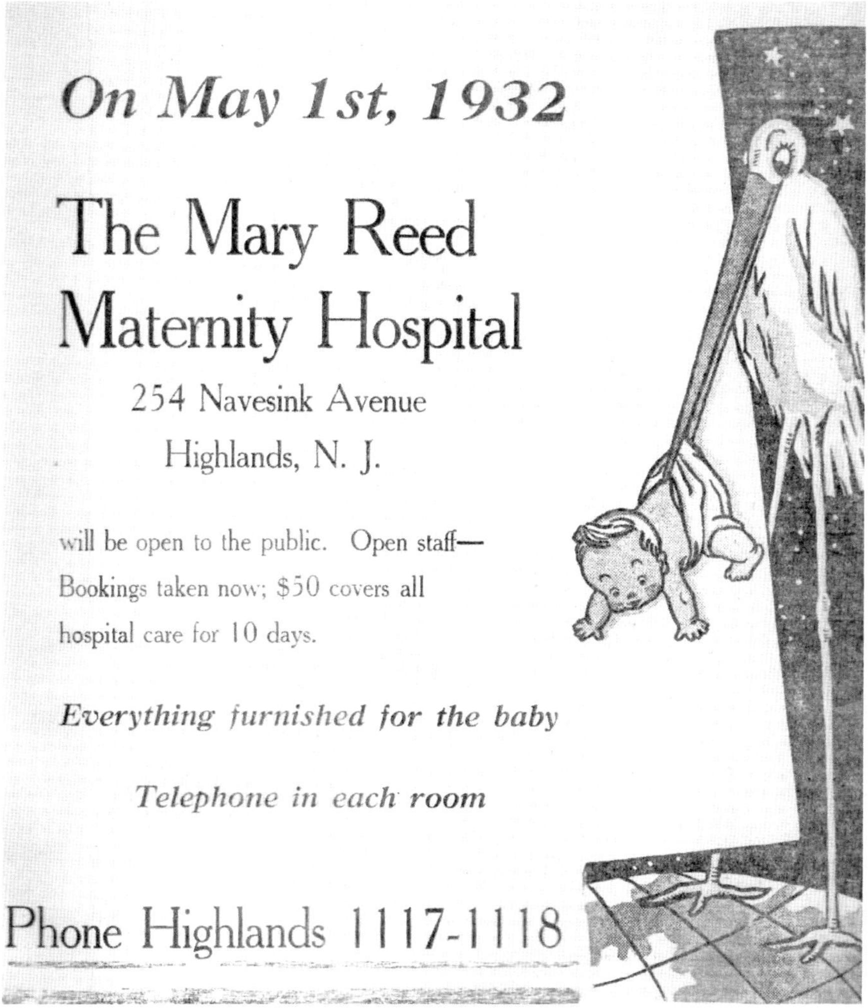

Mary Reed actually started her hospital in a wood-frame house close to Miller Street, the old Duvale house that burned down. This catching full-page ad played in all the area newspapers.

Not all babies we cared for there were born there. Dr. Reed took in some special cases, at times. Once a poor baby was born at home in Parkertown; Dr. Opfermann saw that it was not long to live, having what he called spina bifida, where the spine and cord is exposed. Dr. Reed cared for that poor baby like it was her own, personally feeding, changing and dressing it in sanitary cloths. She lived just three days.

The Dr. Mary Reed Maternity Hospital, after being a rooming house and private home over the years, was the Water Witch House Bed and Breakfast from 1992 to 2002, run by the editor of this book, John P. King, and his wife, Helen.

Another thing that made the hospital come to a close was the ambulance with the new First Aid Squad in town and the Red Bank Hospital. Now women could go to the hospital when their labor started and have their babies, though some still had babies right at home.

—Margaret Peters

IN COURT

Ronald Horan was Municipal Court Judge in Highlands for over fifteen years and presided over two other municipal courts in Monmouth County.

About the people in Highlands, I would say you have people that are quite wealthy and you have people who are unfortunate, maybe, without a great deal of material items of wealth. Both basically good people. You have highly educated people and people with no formal education. But at one time, Highlands was all, well…I'd have to be stupid not to say so…it was getting to the point where sometimes you'd be ashamed to say you lived in Highlands. It was the result of the Depression. People had lost their homes in the city and they were without money. They moved into the summer bungalows and the area did go down. But now, thank God, the town's coming up. We're getting a mixed strata of people. Those families up at the Twin Lights condos and East Pointe—those people naturally are more affluent than most of the people down on Fourth St., Fifth St.

In court I have faced several clamming cases. Sometimes I think the clammers are harassed to the point where some of the rules and requirements are unreasonable. I'm partial to clammers. So the State got to the point where if there was a clamming violation in Highlands or Sea Bright, they wanted to take it to Freehold and not have Horan try it. But I had one case. The clammers were working in a restricted area, I think it was after sundown, they were doing everything wrong. And they were nasty to the Marine Police, extremely nasty in court. When I walked out of court, the defendant's son was standing in the hallway and said, "You're a thief." So I held him in contempt. They had to be held up in Freehold, and he was convicted. They're nasty people. They have no respect for anybody's rights but their own.

There was also a Negro population in Keyport, which we didn't have in Highlands. You see, human nature's the same all over or maybe basically human nature is the same, but there are different groups, different ethnic groups. These think differently. You have to attempt to think the way they think to try and figure out their mores, folkways. To help, not to hurt. But we don't have many of those people in the Highlands yet. Maybe someday we will. Years back there never have been blacks, colored people, in the Highlands. I heard some sordid stories about years and years ago, before I was born, about people being thrown out of town.

—Ron Horan, from an interview by Richard Maxson Jr.

Homesick

Going on this nostalgia trip to the Shrewsbury, the ocean, and the area of the Highlands has made me terribly homesick. There is nothing I want more than to see and smell the river, the ocean once more before I die. I don't know how that will be accomplished as I can't get in and out of a car. An added bonus would be a meal of some clam fritters and some pan fried snapper blues, whole not filleted—the old fashioned way. Boy, I sure have a good case of homesickness!

—Elizabeth S. Smith

The Highlands Ain't the Highlands Anymore!

The Highlands ain't the Highlands anymore,
Oh, the Highlands ain't the Highlands anymore.

They come with big money each month on the first,
From Ft. Hancock they march, soldiers and coast guards galore.
They feel up our daughters, drinking beers for their thirst.
Well, the Highlands ain't the Highlands anymore,
No, the Highlands ain't the Highlands anymore.

New government, water, and electricity too,
Good jobs, boom times like seen never before.
The town's changing for good, a real pleasure to view,
But the Highlands ain't the Highlands anymore,
No, the Highlands ain't the Highlands anymore.

From the cities up north, steam boats, trolleys, long trains,
Now automobiles with grunts, honks, and uproars,
Filthy outsiders all, come causing us pains,
Say, the Highlands ain't the Highlands anymore,
No, the Highlands ain't the Highlands anymore.

Highlands' Miller and Burdge, Parker, Cottrell and Brown,
Maxson, Matthews, and Mount, Liming, Hartsgrove, and Worth,
Now Lynch, Scalia, Rosenblum, Irish, Guinea, and Jew.
Damn, the Highlands ain't the Highlands anymore,
No, the Highlands ain't the Highlands anymore.

—Anonymous
Internal evidence suggests a date around 1910

Our Town

Just a quiet spot in Jersey, by the river and the sea,
And the right amount of neighbors, just enough for you and me;
And it's been this way for quite awhile.
We're not much for stuffy, haughty style,

Though class stands out in all respects
And leaves no one with true regrets.

They say some folks far out at sea
Will gaze our shores in ecstasy,
To see far out on dreary nights
A welcome home from our Twin Lights.
This beacon known through out the world
Has been a signal, once unfurled, to those far out
For some who fear that hope nearby is ever near.

Our men who fish from shore to sea
Bring back the best for all to see.
For no town serves a finer meal,
Than God provides from rake or rod and reel.

But flood tides sometimes far too high,
Invade our town from seas nearby
And we who care, and sometimes shout,
Remember all who are about
And each is cared for, in its way,
And all protected day by day,
Until the floods have left our shore
And anxious neighbors fear no more.

Though few in Highlands have a claim
That ever will reach real fame,
We're very proud of one great star
Whose deeds were miles and miles afar,
A lovely lass, who can forget?
Who brought us fame with records set.
The English Channel was her goal,
Some said a very foolish role,
But swim she did, the world did see,
With Victory as her destiny.
Gertrude Ederle was her name,
Who brought to Highlands worldwide fame.

And now today, near Twin Lights' arc
We've set aside a lovely park
To dedicate to one so grand
A thank you from a grateful band
Of simple folks in a happy town
To Trudy who never let us down.

And now a prayer for those not here
Who helped us build in yesteryears
This town, this land we love so much,
Who cater to the common touch,
Our thoughts, from each and everyone,
A simple Thanks for a job well done.

—Charles B. O'Connor, 1975

Conclusion

Roses in December

The memories of the children, of co-workers, friends and relatives that I have known have enriched my life and left me a wealth of memories of their love, help, thoughtfulness, caring and respect they have accorded me over the years.

I'm sure we all wonder, once in a while, if our lives have made much difference in the world. Have we done all we could to help our fellow travelers along? It's a sobering thought. I too often wonder about this. Friends tell me that I've had a most successful career and have many friends. Sometimes I feel that isn't enough.

At such times I dig into my box of memories and pull out a letter from a little black girl who wrote, "You taught me to love birds. I never even knew that they were there until you taught me to know them." Then for a while at least I feel justified in living. Thank you, Cynthia, wherever you are.

My box is so packed with memories that it is flowing over. It will be of no use to anyone coming after me. But then again they won't have to unpack it and store it away either. It has sustained me under some very trying times and I am grateful for it. I do not know what lies ahead or what losses I may have, but, please, God, let me keep my memories. They are priceless. I thank God everyday, for God gave us memories so that we could have roses in December.

—Ann McNeill

The Highlands

Our town is small
Just one square mile
But it is rumored
That if you dare
Allow its beach sand
In your shoes
You'll fall beneath
Its spell—forever.
Soon you will find
You must return
Time after time.

—Ann McNeill, 1992

About the Editor

John P. King, the editor of this work, has obviously gotten some of the historical sands of Highlands into his shoes, for in his writings he has returned to Highlands time after time. This, his fifth published book on Highlands history, has proved to him to be his most enjoyable, for it gives voice to the very people who made the town the delightful place it once was and still is today. At least two other works on Highlands remain in his computer—one a historical novel, the other a history of the town's first hundred years, thus proving the truth of Ann McNeill's little poem.

King had lived in Highlands some ten years with his wife, Helen, and children, residing in the Dr. Mary Reed hospital, which became their Water Witch House Bed and Breakfast and which prompted his research and writing on Highlands. He developed his historical writing skills as a teacher (now retired) of Latin and French for thirty years at Red Bank Regional High School. He is always deeply grateful to the people of Highlands for their generosity in sharing its history with him and for their kind support and appreciation of his writings.